Sunshine Girl"
By
Carol Morfitt Welch

Presented by:
Brede Publishing

Helping Aspiring Authors Self-publish On Amazon &
Kindle
109 Hialeah Street, Osceola, Wisconsin 54020
715-417-3027
Email   brede.publishing@aol.com

https://www.createspace.com/6934661

ISBN/EAN13:
1543118291 / 9781543118292

Publishing date Feb. 14, 2017

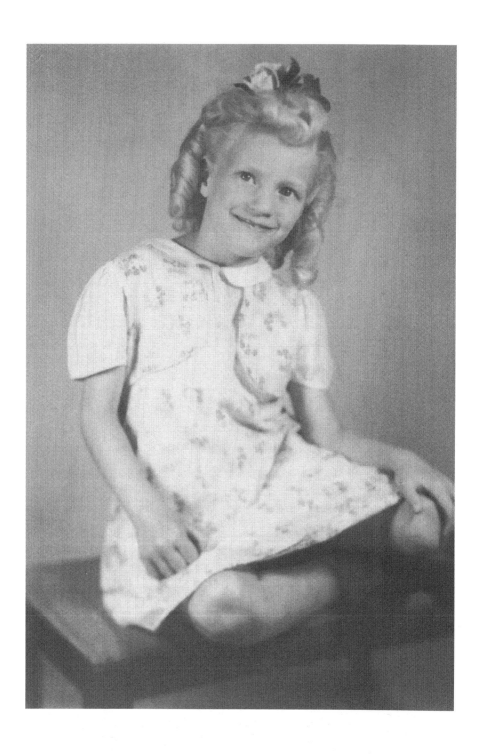

"Sunshine Girl"

By

Carol Morfitt Welch

Edited by,

Joanne Bass

Acknowledgments

I owe thanks to the wonderful Creator who placed me in a world of so many facets.

To the older relatives, many now gone, who gave us hospitality and cousins to enjoy.

To the schools and neighborhoods that fostered growth in our lives.

To Mama who taught me compassion and a love of nature.

To Daddy who shared his witty humor and big heart.

To my daughter, Joanne, who has taken of her precious writing time to lovingly edit this book and encourage me.

To my other four children, Gene, Connie, Russell, and Scott and dear friends who have encouraged my writing.

To a loving Father God Who has allowed insights to grow out of many challenges.

Carol Morfitt Welch

Introduction

Sunshine Girl is the story of generations of hopes and dreams, joys and sorrows, challenges, victories, and disappointments lived out in the life of a young girl in the mid nineteen hundreds.

Northwestern Wisconsin was a collage of farms, quietly ebbing into the age of industrialization, as new mechanical farm equipment slowly began to replace hand tools for farm work. Small towns served the needs of the farm communities and their own working population.

Families recovering from the depression and the First World War were modernizing a bit, many just a step beyond what their immigrant parents had established. German or Scandinavian families composed much of the rural communities, with their industrious lifestyles. Social life centered on the church and rural school.

While the social life in the German community often centered around the local tavern, the Scandinavian community was less open about their usage of beer and wine, and it was more of a personal choice than a cultural norm. There was, however, a different "elixir" that flowed through our Sunshine Girl's family—the fluid ebb and flow of dreams and nature, soaking up the atmosphere of the family farm, and the love and expectations of consideration for others.

The country school, a limited number of schoolmate girlfriends, her brothers, and the farm animals that became her pets were objects of her affection. She learned from her kind-hearted Mama and Daddy about respect and regard for others, though, as the youngest of four, she may have pushed privilege a bit.

As you read Sunshine Girl's story, you will understand that the "simpler life" was just as intricate as life today. Life then, as now, was built on heritage, relationships, ideals, differences, and all the components of society. Through Sunshine Girl you will catch a glimpse into the beautiful tapestry of life and all the factors that bring us to various perceptions and decisions in life. And you will surely find yourself in at least one incident or another, one joy, one heartache, one victory, or one disappointment.

Table of Contents

1 Days of Joy

Warp and weft of life,
not taut or slack,
blend the hues
of furrowed field or track.

Carol trotted barefoot in the warm dust of the driveway,
hurrying to the plowed and harrowed cornfield, where Daddy
was waiting for another small sack of seed corn. Daddy raised
seed corn to supplement the family's dairy income, and the
special seed that Carol carried was for the male rows—the
first two rows out of ten that would pollinate the seed corn.

There was another, greater (in Carol's eyes, at least) element of
her mission. She was the one privileged to deliver to Daddy
the announcement that Citation had won the Kentucky Derby.
While this bit of news may not have been the most important
event in the lives around her, she knew Daddy was waiting to
hear. And to Carol, almost school age and the youngest in the
family, bringing the news to Daddy was a chance to make her
important in Daddy's eyes.

Her announcement proclaimed, Carol followed Daddy to the
corn planter. She watched him carefully remove every kernel
of seed corn as he exchanged it for the corn she had brought. It
was important that the male corn seed not be contaminated.

As Carol watched Daddy carefully remove and replace the precious seed corn, her eyes took in the patient, gray work horses, Bud and Babe, their big crescent-shaped hooves leaving their mark in the deeply worked soil, just waiting. She imagined Citation's hard, fleet hooves gobbling up the turf on the faraway race track. Scenes of riding one of these horses in that swift contest swirled in Carol's mind.

Lifted by the joy of Daddy's approval, the warm May weather, and the presence of horses and land, Carol's heart was running over. The mission to Daddy completed, Carol skipped back to Mama at the house, attempting to match her bare footprints with those of the horses on the dusty driveway.

Those were days of joy for a little blond-haired Wisconsin farm girl. Three older brothers still thought she was a little doll, and Mama called her 'sunshine girl,' although all who knew her were aware that it was very chatty and inquisitive sunshine.

Three brothers, Dane, Jimmy, and LeRoy, though often doting and indulgent, could also be mischievous in ways Daddy and Mama wouldn't have endorsed. There was an unspoken understanding that Carol would not get them in trouble, especially if it seemed they were letting her in on 'big kid' things. (Although the boys were only eight, nine, and ten at this time, they were so big and grown up in Carol's eyes.) So, when they convinced her that she couldn't start school until she was able to hang on to the electric fence, not just on low setting, but high—well, school was wildly desired—her parents did not hear about it, at least not until years later.

Summer days passed quickly, and that wonderful privilege of going to school, first grade, was quickly a reality. Clover Leaf School was a one room school, where eight grades were taught by one teacher. Carol's first grade teacher was heaven-sent. She was a friend of Mama's and a very kind and pleasant teacher. Besides that, her daughter Marlys was Carol's age, and although Marlys attended school in another district, she and Carol played together in the fall leaves and then in the winter snow.

2 Third Horse

What threads we choose
or just receive
produce the tapestry
we weave.

Mama was a plump lady, a little above average height, with a full bosom, a warmth that invited the cuddling of children, a glowing, peaches-and-cream complexion, and kind deep blue eyes. She usually dressed in a flowered house dress, with an apron, if she was cooking or gathering garden vegetables or eggs. On went her denim jacket and a scarf when she would go out to help with chores.

Carol loved to hear Mama tell stories about the early days of her married life with Daddy (Clarence Watrud). It was such fun to hear about those earlier times when Mama was a new wife, working things out with a new husband and community.

Well, Clarence was a wiry young man, muscular, but very slim. He had a shock of brown hair and an expressive face that broke into a broad grin, along with his witty remarks, or set with firmness over an important issue by turns.

After marriage Daddy and Mama took up residence on Clarence's father's farm near Rice Lake, Wisconsin. A cherished part of their living there was the closeness of neighbors, Mike and Sophie Roan, first generation immigrants and farmers. They were long time neighbors of Clarence's parents and took a parent-figure sort of role, humorously endearing and ready with advice and encouragement. Both Mike, with his deeply creased forehead and cheeks, tall and powerfully built, and Sophie, taller than average, with a forward inclined, interested posture, were endearing in a rustic, straightforward way. They also were very bright and had a treasure of history to share if one could take the time to listen, and, of course, if these very industrious people had the free time to give. But, always hospitable, Mike and Sophie would share the time, both to talk and to listen.

Both Mike and Sophie were pleasant, but with no-nonsense appearance and attitudes. Daddy recalled an incident years later in a moment of humorous openness shared with his children: Mike had caught Clarence, who, as a young boy, was trying his hand at smoking a cigar behind the bushes. "Just finish your smoke, son", Mike knowingly advised, and the coughing that followed ended the smoking.

The incident Mama (Ida) recalled from those early days, when Mike and Sophie were their mentors, was remembered as "the solution of the third horse":

Mike and Sophie had a little rat terrier named Buddy, that followed Mike up and down the field as he drove his team of horses, plowing, disking, or cultivating. Tiny Buddy could be seen trotting along, leaping to clear a clod left by the plow, and trotting along again, erect ears alternately showing up and then dropping from view. Clarence and Ida jokingly called him the Roan's "third horse."

Well, Mike and Sophie truly were mentors, nurturing the young couple with encouragement and friendship, but sadly, the peace was severed when the Watruds' cows got into Sophie's prize garden. Occupied with other concerns, Clarence and Ida failed to notice the wandering cows and bring them home quickly.

When Mike strode in angrily, and Sophie turned her back on the couple, it seemed the precious relationship was gone forever. No smiles in passing or friendly chats by the mailbox.

Weeks passed, and the fields had sprouted into rows of corn and oats. One day as Mike was out cultivating his corn, no little black-and-white dog shadowed him. Too proud and miffed to ask for help, Mike and Sophie searched frantically on foot to find their little pet. Their strained voices were faintly heard across the fields, calling, "Buddy...here, Buddy."

Later in the evening, Mama heard a noise near the door, and she opened it to a very dirty and limping little Buddy. She had no idea what had happened to him, but he must have been too traumatized to make it home.

Mama picked up the little wanderer and tended to his injuries. As she cleaned him off, she thought hopefully of the joy that Mike and Sophie would feel, knowing he was—nearly—all right. Mama set her apron aside and put on her wool plaid jacket, eager to return the prodigal pet.

Mama walked apprehensively across the field and up to the house, reflecting on the recent coldness. She knocked on the door, and Mike and Sophie appeared together. "I've brought your 'third horse' back," Mama said with all the cheerfulness she could muster.

There were healing smiles all around, and folks who weren't accustomed to hugging, hugged. Clarence came in from the field, dusty and fatigued, to the good news that their dear neighbors were reconciled to them, thanks to a little "third horse."

3 Empty Arms

The river flows
past rocks and trees,
like colored strands
for tapestries.

Ida was a mother; that was for sure. The excitement of awaiting their first baby seemed to motivate her to do the super-human. While Clarence worked hard, getting the farm operation going as well as working part time in a canning factory to make ends meet, Ida worked too—harder than she should have. She milked the cows as needed, fed and cleaned for a growing little flock of chickens, and cared for their pigs—a boar and two brood sows.

No one ever knew for sure whether it was the pigs or the handling of hay machinery that caused the trouble. While Clarence was at work at the canning factory, one of the brood sows got out, and Ida dashed out to chase her back to the pen. The sow went wild, and the more Ida chased her, the harder she ran, until the two of them stood exhausted and gasping. Breath recovered, Ida was finally able to get the pig back into her pen and fasten the fence just in time for the beginning of the birth of the pig's litter.

Clarence arrived home to a settled scene, all livestock in their places, and new piglets being birthed without problems. But that day wasn't over yet.

Rain was threatening, and there was a load of hay that hadn't yet been put into the haymow. Clarence harnessed the horses while Ida got the wagon ready to be hitched. Another partly loaded small trailer stood in front of the wagon, and Ida raised up on it to roll it out of the way. Finding it heavier than she anticipated, she lifted harder, but she immediately felt a sharp stab of pain. Ida instinctively felt that something serious had occurred.

When Clarence pulled up with the horses, Ida quietly helped him move the trailer, not mentioning the fear and pain she was experiencing. He hitched the horses up to the hay wagon to pull the hay under a lean-to by the barn to keep it dry.

Checking on the mother pig and her little ones and warming a light snack for bedtime ended that long day, but the night that followed wasn't a restful one for Ida. While Clarence was quickly snoring as soon as his head hit the pillow, Ida lay awake with sharp pains along with a painful stab of fear.

Before many hours, the severity of her pain and the bleeding that progressed caused her to wake Clarence. As he attempted to help her stand, the tiny fetus was expelled, and their first baby was gone.

Ida's parents and sisters drove the fifty miles to come and see her. In answer to their concern, she said she was all right, but "My arms feel so empty."

Clarence always thought the miscarriage was caused by the chasing of the ornery pig, but Ida must have thought it was the lifting, because years later she warned her daughter never to over-lift because it can hurt your childbearing organs.

Clarence told his little daughter that her sister—the baby they had lost—would have been named Ramona. However, when choosing names for each of the three boys who followed Ramona, the feminine name would have been Lois. The boys, of course, were given masculine names, but when the daughter finally came, she was called Carol.

The year following was one of drought, waiting for rain to sprout the oats, only to watch them shrivel, then waiting for rain to sprout the planted rows of corn, and watching that shrivel as well. The pastures didn't green up with grass, and most farmers had used up last year's hay. Driven by desperation to feed their livestock, farmers cut tree branches that, fortunately, had leafed out and cut weeds that always seem hardier than crops. Many farmers herded their cattle into the north woods, where there was, at least, foliage they could hope would be enough to keep their animals alive.

Some cattle were butchered, but since there were no freezers, the meat had to either be canned or used immediately. Ida treasured her canner and appropriated all the jars she could get and boiled them full of meat for hour after hour.

When it was apparent that all the possible crops had failed, farmers contacted farms in other parts of the country where the drought was less severe and ordered hay they hoped would be available.

"The cows don't even bellow now," Clarence reported." They are getting thinner and thinner, picking among twigs or whatever they can get hold of for a bite to eat." The special cows with which Clarence was starting his herd, were still alive, but gaunt, feeble near-skeletons, who could elicit no feeling but pity.

"Ida, even our foundation cows are near death. Maybe I should take them out of their misery." As Clarence pondered whether to shoot them, news came from neighbors. Trucks of hay were on their way!

There was no guarantee that animals so near starvation could revive, but farmers started feeding their starving animals sparsely at first, not to shock their systems and also, because they didn't know how long the precious feed would last or if more was available. Clarence often told, over the years, how he marveled that those starving cows stoically kept silent, but when feed arrived, they bellowed incessantly.

Two years into their marriage, with the loss of the baby, anxiety, and the austerity necessary to survive, the couple looked at future possibilities. Even the canning factory hadn't produced, so money was lacking; but, as the year progressed, Ida had a secret growing deep within her. If God willed this, He would give every reason to hope.

4 Moving On

Do snarls in yarn
the image blur,
or Providence
make pattern sure?

Many changes—family needs and expectations, declining health of Clarence's mother, another brother wishing to farm solo—brought about the move to a rental farm forty-five or fifty miles away. This turned out to be a farm near Ida's "home place," and she always referred to this farm as the Lien Place.

The cows that Clarence had earned during high school years and after, through his work at the Achtenberg farm, and calves those cows had borne were moved to the rental farm. The cows had been named after the Achtenberg daughters, Bonnie and Jackie. Other cows were named by their appearance: Ducky, Bluebell, Princess, Lady, etc., and the calves were given names beginning with the first letter of the mother cow's name.

Things like rickety fences, building repairs, and getting the fields tilled to produce crops were the first tasks at hand. No longer having his father's machinery to work with, Clarence had to buy, borrow or trade to procure enough implements to do his field work. Fortunately, they lived nearer to Ida's family and relatives, so sometimes a dear uncle or cousin would lend a piece of machinery or help put the hay in the barn before a rain.

Unlike the flat land of the Watrud family farm they had just moved from, the Lien place was situated in a hilly area; and Ida enjoyed the beauty of it, writing poems and doing sketches of her surroundings.   However, she was a woman who worked side by side with her husband, rebuilding those rickety fences, working in the field and garden, and milking the cows. That left little time for creativity in the present, but she was destined to share that love of nature and expression with children still to come.

It was on this farm that their first son was born. Ida often enjoyed telling how at the time of the baby's birth she got a chance to one-up her husband, who was a witty young man with a love for telling a good joke.

Clarence, ever the hard worker, often worked late into the evening on the farm in addition to working at the canning factory in the summer. Consequently, he was slow to get up mornings. Ida, always the early riser, would smile her gentle smile accompanied by a good-natured wink when mentioning his getting up. She would call him, sometimes more than once, and then they would start the chores.

On this day, it was Ida who hadn't gotten up, and she whispered, "I think it's time." Clarence was out of bed, dressed, had the horses hitched, and was on his way to get her sister who was to help with the birth, before Ida was even able to tell him how long she thought it might be.

It was a happy day, and everyone rejoiced over the wiggly little curly-haired blond baby. Ida's precious secret finally lay in her arms—Dane Robert Watrud!

Two cousins stayed to help until Ida got back on her feet, and the joy of tending to her darling baby— dressing him in the clothing she had been sewing, knitting, and crocheting after chores in the evening— was healing and newness all at once. "I felt like I was playing house," she later recalled, "wheeling him in the wicker buggy we received as a gift." She also recalled with fondness her uncles, Ole J. and Ole R. Flaa visiting and giving her special figurines as keepsakes.

Ida's father, a big man with a full mustache and frank blue eyes, treasured the new baby and was teary with thankfulness that his daughter had come through with such happiness. Ida had been the daughter who had paddled along after him as a little girl, helping him with the chores and never needing correction, except for once when she repeated what he said to a naughty sheep. Then, as a teenager, Ida had stayed home and helped her mother while her sister went away to Rice Lake for high school.

Ida later went to work in her older sister's store in Iowa, much to her mother's dismay and father's pain of parting. Now, here she was, holding a baby son. Yes, it did warm his heart.

Ida's mother, who had raised seven babies herself, took it in stride, reminding Ida of basic procedure. This made Ida smile to herself, as she had frequently cared for other people's babies before marrying Clarence.

The first day of October was the top of the world. Celebrating the new baby, and then Grandpa Hanson's (Ida's father) birthday on October second, made it one of the best times for all.

The beginning of October was also time of harvest. The corn had done well on the Lien place, diligently fertilized with cow manure and what commercial fertilizer could be afforded. Little Dane in his buggy soon became as much at home in the barn during milking time as he was in the lean-to shed while Ida husked corn. With hay and grain stored for the winter and Clarence's faithful cows prospering, it looked like a good year.

5 Rocky Fields and Neighbors

A single thread
with more entwines;
in joy, in tears,
forms its designs.

Life on the Lien place had been a new start for Clarence and Ida, and now little Dane was growing, cooing, and generally being the light of his parents' lives. . There were, however, hints that the new daddy sometimes found himself displaced by the new little resident, especially when bouts of colic in the early months kept Ida occupied with comforting Dane for hours at a time. Still, all in all, they later recalled those as happy months, especially due to the usual progression of colic to lessen after the first three or so months.

While little Dane was recovering from colic and growing a head of enviable shining gold curls, mornings became progressively difficult for Ida. Normally the bright early riser, nausea began to slow her down and zap her energy. She who had always initiated morning chores now did them prodded only by her responsible nature to do her share.

With Ida busy as always and now not feeling well on top of it, summer came and Clarence went back to work at the canning factory. Drought and the depression had changed the economy; and while it brought much devastation, it also brought a type of relief to Ida—help in the home! Many young or elderly people whose families' finances had all but diminished made themselves available to help in the home or farm for room and board and a few necessities.

Thus, Gerena, an elderly distant relative, came to live in the Watrud home, freeing Ida for a few hours at a time to help with the haying, milk the cows while Clarence went to his job at the canning factory, and to keep up the garden and can vegetables for the following winter.

A believer in the necessity of a good farm dog to round up cattle, Clarence brought home a speckled and spotted black on white and gray mixed-breed puppy. "That black spot on his tongue," Clarence's veterinarian father announced, "means he has the makings of a good cow dog."

Clarence was a sensible and methodical dog trainer, but not afraid to correct vigorously when commands weren't followed. So the little dog they had named Pepper was beginning to get the idea of chasing the cows into the barn and was beginning to accompany Ida in bringing the cows in from the pasture, moving lagging cows and giving them motivation to stay in motion.

As winter approached, there were less days in the pasture, and Pepper could be more of a pet.

Little Dane, now approaching a year old, learned to pet him gently and not to pull his hair and tail, and not to grab for the quick little spotted tongue. With supervision, the dog was rather good company for the little toddler. A fairly long-haired dog, Pepper was comfortable outside and would sleep on the porch or just inside the front door, as the family and weather dictated.

A male dog, Pepper was likely to stray if there were any female dogs in the area. Clarence kept an eye on him, and any suspicious behavior would have Pepper sleeping inside the house. One night, however, when Pepper was neither at the front door wagging his tail nor responding to their calls. Clarence drove the rickety old Dodge pickup through the neighborhood, calling for Pepper. Finally Clarence resigned himself to the fact that he wouldn't find his little dog that night, and he went home to bed.

Ida was awakened the following morning by a moaning at the door. She hurriedly opened it, finding Pepper broken and dragging his hind quarters. Clarence joined Ida and saw that his back was broken and his hind quarters cruelly bloodied. Retrieving his rifle from the closet, Clarence picked up the broken dog, carried him behind the shed, and the report of the rifle ended his moans.

"Whoever did this should have just penned his female dog and warned me," Clarence couldn't conceal his rage. "They could have done what others have always done—roughened his back end, painted it with turpentine, and sent him on his way. That miserable discomfort always discourages further visits." And an embittered young man buried his would-have-been cow dog.

But life went on, Clarence cooled down, and new opportunity came. "Ida, Ida! A farm is coming up for sale east of Clear Lake," Clarence happily shouted as he rushed into the kitchen.

This idea was new to Ida who had spent the past year working to decorate the rented house and make it homey, arranging the bedroom to accommodate a new bassinet and a place in the adjoining room where little Dane's crib would be convenient and warm.

Needless to say, a time of discussion was needed before the possibilities, the necessary arrangements and work made sense. "Well, what is the house like? The neighborhood? The farm buildings? Can we afford it?"

An enthusiastic young man saw possibilities in every aspect of the venture. "It's pretty level land, and the owners need to sell. There's a usable barn and an adequate house, a well, and a partial fence with a lane. A pretty little creek crosses the driveway, and the neighbors are friendly. It's near the Moe church on a beautiful hill. You'll love it."

Ida looked at her handiwork, the curtains fashioned of print flour and chicken feed sacks she had collected. "Not a bad-looking decorating scheme," she thought, and her eyes strayed to the bedroom, where the white ruffled items she had collected through the years as she dreamed of a new daughter had begun to accumulate. The little bluish enamel wood burning cook stove with the oven door that needed propping up, the wash stand, and cupboard that Clarence had built all added to her feeling of home. It would take some thought to adjust to the idea of possibly moving again.

6 Neighborly Smiles

The plan in strand,
thread intricate,
an image tells
its trend or fate.

Clarence began to share solid facts and figures as he talked, still eagerly, about the possibility of a new farm. "We would actually be the owners, and improvements we make would increase our net worth."

Full of questions, Ida listened to her husband's dreams. "How could we undertake a move with another baby on the way? How would we get buildings and fences ready for cows?" Ida also had questions about necessary energy and provisions.

Reassurance came as Clarence talked about possible times for the needed steps to be taken. First, he had to be assured of financial backing. Then, he would determine the logistics of keeping his canning factory job along with repairing and setting up a new farm system. The piece of news most helpful to Ida was that, if everything else was favorable, an actual move couldn't take place until about the first of April, when it was customary for the ownership or tenancy of farms to change hands. According to her reckoning, late December would be the date for the birth of Dane's new little sibling.

Activities on the Lien place settled down to a more normal routine. Ida experienced her burst of energy after early pregnancy nausea had passed. There were the new calves to be fed, daily chores, and cooking the delicious meals she had come to be known for. Little Dane was a joy, quickly expanding his repertoire of short words and expressions.

Life was full for Ida. Little Dane supplied a fair amount of laundry to scrub on the washboard and rinse in the galvanized tubs. Her treadle Singer sewing machine, a loan from her parents, was often heard turning out clothing for the new baby on the way. Her mind was on a girl, but the type of newborn garments didn't matter so much, because in the early 1930's both boys and girls wore dresses or gowns the first year or so. Dane, however, had graduated to pants and shirts, and that was another sewing job to accomplish.

Clarence took advantage of the late fall and early winter months to get his ducks in a row for the hoped-for upcoming change of farms. He approached finance agencies and farm program representatives, and he visited the farmers in the community to get acquainted and get a feel for the practices in the area. His forays on the potential farm disclosed a feature that would impact the nature of the farm work.

Rows of rock piles skirted the fields, and not having been farmed for a year or two, rocks were scattered generously on the surface. "Well, he thought, if I can swing the deal, rocks are not going to stand in my way."

On one of his outings, Clarence saw the opportunity to once again have a cattle dog. One of the local farmers he spoke to had a beautiful white purebred collie with a litter of puppies. "Well. Clarence," he said, "if it wasn't for irresponsible dog owners, we would have a purebred litter, worth a good price; but she has mated with a stray, and I'll be lucky to give the puppies away. Of course," he admitted, "female dogs do need to be confined to avoid unwanted mating."

The gist of this conversation was that Clarence had the opportunity to choose among the puppies what he hoped would be a future cow dog He picked a white puppy with a dark brown head, alert, slightly forward tipped ears, and a broad white stripe from the back of his head to his black nose tip. A large black patch on the middle of his back broke up his snow white coat.

Clarence had no doubt Ida would be as delighted and hopeful as he. It was in an elated frame of mind that he hurried home in time for supper and evening chores, with this new little friend and responsibility, who might add to the success of their farming venture. 'You'll do fine, little lad," He tucked the puppy beside him in the old pickup. As he was rewarded with a kiss on the hand by a warm little tongue. A black spot on the puppy's tongue. "Yes," he said, "I think you'll make a fine cow dog."

Ida met Clarence with her warm smile, enhanced by the bloom of healthy pregnancy and the tantalizing aroma of an artfully seasoned supper. Happily he reached underneath his Mackinaw jacket and held up for her approval the wiggly, white puffball.

Approval came in abundance, and Ida quickly found a peach crate, just right to line with an old blanket scrap for a bed for the puppy.

Thanks to Gerena's presence. Ida had been able to leave little Dane long enough to feed the cows, so they were ready to sit down to a hot meal after appropriately and lovingly cuddling and welcoming the new resident.

The usual conversations when Clarence returned from his fact-finding and negotiating expeditions were set aside as a name was sought for the puppy, efforts were made to keep a wiggly toddler corralled in his high chair, and praise and thanks were offered for these blessings. "I've kind of been calling him Lad," Clarence offered. "He is a little boy."

"Laddie," Ida joined in. "It's a beautiful name. It sounds like a Scotch collie, although he is a white collie—and whatever else you said his paternal lines might be." It was approved by all, including Gerena; and little Dane remarked, "Wow-wow."

So life began with a new family member. Routines included housebreaking the little fellow. Clarence vowed, "I'll never have a dog worth its salt sleeping outdoors, regardless of the opinions of others." The brutal loss of one pet/helper confirmed the resolution to protect his right hand helper-to-be, whatever effort it required.

"He'll learn house manners soon enough," Ida agreed, showing Laddie his sleeping box and coaching little Dane in the way to treat a puppy. An eager wet muzzle poked onto the toddler's hand, bringing giggles. Ida sighed, thinking of the training to follow. "It's a while to spring," she reflected, "and Laddie has time to grow up a little before learning to herd cows." In the meantime, she would cheerfully take the extra housework in stride.

Weeks passed, and the progress toward buying the farm moved along. Clarence was eager to have Ida meet the hopefully-soon-to-be neighbors. Across the road from the farm they hoped to buy were the Ericksons who had one little boy, about two years older than Dane. They were warmly welcoming and Mrs. Erickson—Sal—in her humorous, bordering-on-blunt way, filled Ida in on the location of the neighboring farms and the personalities of their residents. With Sal's kindly verbal caricatures, Ida anticipated enjoying getting acquainted with others. "Most of the ladies go to the Moe Church sewing circle every month," Sal remarked, "And you might like to come even if you haven't decided on the farm. But I sure hope you do become our neighbors."

New thoughts about the farm whirled through Ida's mind. Having grown up in a rural neighborhood, anticipating neighbors all around appealed to her sociable nature. Now the cold winds of November edged toward December snow, and the approaching of the baby's expected arrival prompted preparations in earnest. Linens that were to be on hand for the birthing were sterilized and stored in sterile sheets, and an extra bed was prepared for the special event.

Christmas approached with Ida's extended family, the Hansons, very involved in preparations. Ida had kept knitting needles clicking every spare minute through the late fall, making wool socks for Pa and her four brothers and mittens for her sisters. Her sister Agnes, just two years younger than Ida, who was crippled with rheumatoid arthritis, would be comforted by new warm, wool sleep socks; and Mama would get new potholders and dish towels that Ida embroidered with cheery flowers. She was making Clarence a beautiful plaid flannel shirt to wear with his special suede leather jacket. "He will look so handsome in the blue plaid to match his eyes." she said as she eased her heavy, soon-to-deliver, form into a most welcome bed.

Dane had been lullabied, Laddie firmly settled for the night, and Clarence had drunk his hot cocoa and hit the hay as well. "Getting ready for Christmas and a new baby at the same time is a big order." Ida reminded herself not to set her heart on a girl, although the name, Lois, stayed on her mind. If God blessed them with another healthy baby, she knew she would be content. Ida's sister Christine, and a neighbor who worked as a midwife when needed, were prepared for the call. Since the Watruds didn't yet have a phone, Clarence was especially careful that the old pickup would be ready at a moment's notice, prepared to notify and bring the help.

7 Granddad

Beneath the loom,
rough, tangled thread,
only hint of beauty
overhead.

Tomorrow, December 22, would be Ida's birthday. As close as she could figure, the birth should not be many days off. She felt a warm sense of satisfaction as she mentally rehearsed the preparations she had done ahead for the family Christmas. Candied fruit and orange peels had been dried, ready for her special fruitcake, always in demand; and the root cellar was stocked with potatoes ready to be made into lefse. Pa would, as always, bring the lutefisk, and dried cranberries on the pantry shelf would be cooked into a tart and tasty relish. A couple of large roosters would supply the meat.

As Ida grew more restless, and the sleep she had anticipated after a busy day eluded her, she began to suspect that the birth was to be sooner than it had seemed during the day. She was glad her sister Christine had spent the night and had insisted on setting up a birthing bed with sanitary sheets and water-resistant mattress covers before they went to bed.

Ida hated to wake Clarence hours before morning chore time, but the plans were that he would go to the Blair's and call Dr. Nelson to deliver the baby. "We've got to wake him," Christine argued, noting how quickly Ida's labor was accelerating. Ida, who tended to take discomfort in her stride, was becoming agitated.

"Clarence," Christine called, "the baby's on its way, and you need to get to the Blair's quickly." He rushed out the door, and Christine and Ida listened for the old pickup to start. After a few chugs, it did start, and they got busy preparing Ida for the birth. It seemed the bearing-down pains were coming early in the labor, and nothing was happening after the initial breaking of the waters. Minutes crawled by, then an hour. Clarence returned to say Dr. Nelson was on a call but would come to the Watrud's next.

Christine comforted Ida with cool cloths on her forehead, encouraged her from other labors she had seen, and tried to make sense of the way things were progressing. "Breathe fast. Try not to push." Would the doctor ever arrive?

When there was no let-up between contractions, and Dr. Nelson still hadn't arrived, Christine knew she had to do something. While they had thought the baby would be breach, when she examined her sister, she determined that he was approaching head first; but the front of his head was face up, which could have been life-threatening.

The time to begin chores came and passed. Little Dane wanted attention, and Christine steered him to Gerena, who was a godsend at a time like this. Time became urgent, and Christine, with a prayer in her heart and fear of the alternatives, proceeded with actions she had never taken before. Reassuring Ida, keeping Clarence busy boiling water and bringing clean towels and cloths, she worked to gently steer the baby's face to the side, as she encouraged Ida to try pushing once more.

Little James entered the world, and with a little patting and rubbing, let out a lusty cry, startling his daddy and curly-headed brother, who was itching to get into the room from where that cry was heard.

Clarence rushed into the room, grabbed Ida's exhausted hand and greeted his new son, "Hi, Granddad."

Two cars rumbled into the snowy yard, one after the other. Uncle Hjalmer had finished chores and came to see how Christine was doing; and Dr. Nelson, having finished his emergency house call, came to see how Ida was doing. Dr. Nelson reached down and good-naturedly picked up the fourteen-month-old big brother as he listened to Christine's labor and delivery report.

"Well, it's another fine boy," he commented enthusiastically. "Does this mean the able nurse is ready to join my staff?" Uncle Hjalmer, always ready with a retort, replied, "Would that mean you'd show up the day you're needed?"

Dr. Nelson, used to Hjalmer's churlish ways, laughed it off and turned his attention to Ida's birthday. He wisely did not refer to the girl he knew she had hoped for but saw the mother love and recalled how the Good Book says that the pain of childbirth is forgotten in the joy of new life. "What a birthday gift!" he exclaimed and noticed that Ida's eyes glistened with happy tears.

The Hanson Christmases were always a festive affair, with the married children coming with their babies and the boys at home and little Edna all making presents for one another.

Ida's mother said Ida should be their guest this year, so the goodies were cooked at Ma and Pa's house, with little Edna, now fourteen, absolutely enchanted over the little baby and cute toddler older brother.

The new baby was named James Burnell after two of the Watrud relatives, and the surroundings glowed with the presence of a new baby at Christmas. As they drove home Christmas night in the old pickup, Clarence pondered over family memories, the hard times, the Providence that came through for them, and the promise of Christmas itself. Instead of his customary crash into bed and sleep, after chores, he helped tuck Dane into bed with a prayer he himself learned as a child. "Little star, overhead, looking down on my bed, Can you see God's kind eyes, watching me from the skies?" Seeing Ida had nursed and dressed the new baby for bed, he kissed them both and said to his new son, "Goodnight, Granddad."

8 Willow Creek & Comic Calluses

The vision that saw
plan's motif,
predicting thread above,
beneath.

"I was warned about the rocky fields—and I saw the rocks," Clarence reminded both himself and Ida. "But the pesky hope of actually owning our own farm and the vision of making a go of it deluded me of clear vision." And, if ever there was a way of "making a go of it," this industrious couple applied themselves to it.

Baby Jimmy had fared well with the severe winter, his chubby little wrists and dimpled fingers creased with evidence of his gain. He had also survived the enthusiastic entertainment of his toddler brother Dane. Once, when rollicking giggles sounded from the bedroom where little Jimmy was in his bassinet and Dane was rapidly clicking scissors above his laughing face, Ida spoke calmly. "I'll have to have those scissors now." Needless to say, thorough efforts were made to child proof the house.

The days flew by rapidly now. The contracts on the new farm were almost completed, and Ida's work of leaving the rental home neat and clean occupied much of her time. Keeping up laundry for two babies in diapers and her share of barn chores filled the too few hours of the winter days. The diapers freeze-dried on the clothes lines, brought in stiff to finish drying near the wood heater.

Gerena, though willing and cheerful, was elderly, and her biggest help was to be on hand. After Dane's novel ways on entertaining baby Jimmy, Ida felt it best to bundle Dane up and take him along while she fed cows and calves and helped with milking. She left Gerena in the house with a loud cowbell to ring in case the baby needed immediate care. So it went, with the barn door open, so any signal could be heard.

And with all the heat and moisture generated by the cows, an hour or so of ventilation in the barn proved to be beneficial. Clarence would have the silage and straw dug from their frosty storage and hay thrown down from the haymow for feeding before Ida left to make supper.

An occasional visit with new neighbors was Ida's favorite part of this transition. The farm chores, along with packing up and cleaning the rental home and preparing the new home for living, left Ida very receptive to a few hours of visiting while Clarence went on with plans to ready the buildings and fences for the livestock. Allowances had been made by the lender for Clarence to get stalls and fences repaired, and as new owners the Watruds could be ready to move their property in on April first, the traditional rural moving day. There was some mutual anxiety over whether the little creek that crossed the driveway would flood its banks, knocking out the bridge that led into the farm yard. More than one sigh of relief was breathed when they saw the little creek was down and the thawing past when the Watruds prepared to herd their livestock into their new surroundings.

Laddie had matured a good bit over the winter, and he obediently responded to the orders and signals to move the cows through the six miles of muddy road. Remodeled gates, unfamiliar fence arrangement, and a different farmstead could have made the arrival difficult, but Clarence's hours of training Laddie, the help of neighbors, and calm attitudes made the move as smooth as the driving of a dozen cows, several calves, and a bull led separately on a chain could be.

Again, sighs of relief accompanied the settling of the cows and calves into their stalls and pens. Ida still had her beautiful laying hens and feisty rooster to settle in the makeshift coop adjoining the barn

"I guess the egg and milk production will be down for a few days," Ida commented, remembering past moves and other upsets in routine. Come that as it may, the animals were settled in their abodes while Gerena sat in the partly-furnished house with the two tiny boys. Dane was fascinated enough with all he could see of the activity to be relatively subdued.

"Oh,no! Toto is riled up and threatening to break down his stall." The huge white bull, usually docile, was disturbed by the increased activity of moving cattle. In spite of his heavily reinforced log-built stall, a ring in his nose with a chain tying him to the manger, and a neck strap, his size and agitated state had Clarence and Ida concerned about new quarters.

Reasoning that Toto had been calm and manageable on two different farms, Clarence and Ida worked at calming him with grain, asking those helping to step outside. With the reducing of exciting activity, Toto began to settle down, and Clarence and Ida joined hands and turned to Father God, who had provided this far, to calm Toto and give them wisdom to keep their livestock and home safe. With the safeguard of Toto's nose ring, chain, and tie strap, along with the calmer state of things, the young couple continued the settling in of the household and the milking utensils as a peach and blue-gray April sunset signaled time to thank their help, serve the always ready coffee and rolls, and start evening chores.

Gerena and the helpful neighbor ladies were a blessing, tending to the children so Ida could be "right hand man" during this busy time.

Buoyed up by the prospect of arranging the new house, checking out what could be used from things she had made for the rental house, and having new neighbors that were actually eager to share in her decorating plans, Ida launched out on her new routine. The new house had a little more room for the boys—two bedrooms for the time when she would be ready to move Jimmy out of the bassinet and into a crib in his own room. Would Dane be ready for a big bed by then? She broke into a smile as she thought of the passing of time, changing little Jimmy to a babbler and Dane to a little baby-talker, with new words coming daily. Some were a puzzle to interpret, followed by the fun of figuring it out and sharing with Clarence.

Singing a Swedish song she had learned from Pa, Ida held up her bright kitchen curtain fabric as she whirled around the kitchen. This brought giggles from Dane and a blush to her own cheeks, as at that very moment Clarence entered the door with a neighbor man. "You remember Sal's husband, Lars Erickson. He helped set up the chicken house. I know how special that is to you."

Rising to the occasion, Ida quipped, "Yes, a man after my own heart! That lean-to coop is just perfect for the summer months; with the chickens not needing so much warmth."

Lars made himself at home, and, again, Ida was glad for the move. "Tell Sal I'd like to have her come over whenever she can. I don't know if Lawrence, being almost school age, would think such young boys as ours are fun, but I'll bet we could find something he'd like." Lars chuckled at the enthusiasm and nodded his assent.

With the warming of spring, Clarence worked on machinery to work up the soil and arranged to trade labor for use of machinery the Watruds did not yet own. Cub and Bell, the slow and balky team of horses that had been used on the old Rice Lake farm, were replaced by Snip and King, a half bronco/half draft team that had a tendency to charge forward and needed firm guidance to be kept steady. Clarence picked up and hauled the bountiful rocks out of the field on a stone boat he had made of rough-sawn planks and log skids. Planting couldn't begin until this task was complete.

With the off-farm canning factory job looming, every day took on supreme importance. Rocks had to be removed, fields plowed and disked, and the grain seeder in repair ready to go—and the field work all had to be done while Clarence's hours were available. So, the ridges of rock piles grew along the fencerows as the fields were cleared and tilled. Oat sprouts showed in fresh, green rows, and it was time to plant the corn. Hay machinery needed to be put in good repair, and Clarence made frequent trips to the blacksmith.

At day's end, neighbors up and down the country road would occasionally gather to discuss fieldwork progress, cattle issues, and the exchanging of hired help hours as needs occurred. Again, the availability of youthful or elderly farm help due to the depression enabled many of these farmers, whose children were too young to take on strenuous tasks, to manage productive farms.

One fellow named Ernie worked for various farmers by the day or by the job, sometimes lending a hand at the Watrud farm. Ernie had a peculiarity of not remembering if he had eaten, and some of the farmers made a joke of this. Incensed at such treatment, Ida announced, "No fun at the expense of others in my house."

Laddie, the young white collie was becoming a helpful addition under Clarence's training, and his dark brown ears would stand erect at the mention of cows. To the familiar call, "Come, boss, come, boss," Laddie would head for the lane leading to the cow pasture. Later on, he learned to bring them in by himself, but at this point the big pup was on hand to help keep them moving in the right direction.

Clarence enjoyed visiting with the neighbors when he had errands at their farms, and he was often known to compliment, especially the older ladies, on their current baking results. This, of course, often produced the hoped-for results of earning him a sample. Mable Blair, a confident and quick older lady, responded to one of his "fishing for treats" ploys by giving him a nice, big memorable spoonful of her freshly ground horse radish. True to his indomitable nature, laughing and eyes watering, Clarence choked it down.

A gelding Percheron colt, black, with the promise of growing into a dappled gray, was added to the livestock. He was from a stallion named Tarzan, and Clarence sought out the owner of the stallion to get his bronco mare, Snip, bred, hoping to eventually have a team of grays of powerful Percheron bloodlines.

Summer moved on. The Erickson, the Hummels, the Mitchells, the Pearsons, and many others, worked their crops, visiting in passing, always with the morning or afternoon coffee set out, with apron clad ladies and overall clad men laughing or expressing concerns together.

Clarence's sister, Charlotte (who had been instrumental as matchmaker for Clarence and Ida) and her husband Fred came out for a visit. They were both teachers, and during summer break they would take education courses at the college and then travel before the next school term. Their three children, Bob, Ken, and Jeannette, were a dozen years older than the Watrud children, and Bob asked if they could stay and help with the haying. This became his practice for several years and was a beloved part of the Watrud's summers.

9 Butchering Time

Each strand of design
counted with care,
the heddle lowered
to hold each there.

It may come as no surprise that by the time two crops of hay were harvested, the oats threshed, and tassels appeared on the growing corn, Ida noticed a familiar queasiness and extra fatigue. But with a nursing baby, two sets of diapers to keep laundered, and men to cook for, the discomfort would have had to have been overwhelming to have stopped her from her responsibilities. Nevertheless, it was there.

Once again she brushed aside thoughts of bonnets and ribbons with the onrushing train of tasks that presented themselves day by day.

The piglets they had brought from Lien place had filled out and were ready to butcher or sell. They would need to butcher at least one pig to furnish lard for cooking and, along with a yearling steer, meat to feed the workers. Several neighbors pooled funds and employed a truck to take their pigs to the market at South St. Paul. The extra cash helped take care of the expense of cultivating and harvesting crops.

"Just thinking of butchering that hog," Ida confided in Sal, "makes my stomach churn.

"Don't you worry about it," Sal responded with hearty enthusiasm. "I'll be right there to help."

The hog butchering morning came, and Ida began the day same as always. She got up, got through the battle with the lingering nausea, changed and nursed baby James, and got Dane dressed for the day. She was thankful for Gerena who, though she wasn't up to much exertion, was able to keep one of the boys occupied while Ida cared for the other.

"Dad's here!" Clarence called. His Dad, Joe Watrud, lived thirty miles away and didn't get to Clarence and Ida's often, although being a veterinarian, he was more used to travel than the average farmer. He chatted with Clarence and Ida as they went through the routine of chores— milking the cows, cleaning after them, and setting the milk cans in the freshly pumped water tank to cool.

Offering the always present cup of coffee and rolls, Ida got breakfast on, and then they were ready for the ordeal, as Ida saw it in light of her physical response at this time, of killing and butchering the hog.

A sturdy small diameter beam, often a small single tree, otherwise used for hitching a horse for pulling, was made ready. It was fitted with sturdy hooks at either end, with one in the middle to attach to a heavy rope that would raise it to a pulley fastened to a sturdy scaffold near the barn.

If you have ever heard the expression "like a stuck pig," you have an idea of the next part of the procedure. Fortunately, this part doesn't take long, and it is probably the quickest and most humane way to take the hog from perambulating to being processed into meat. Hooking the hind feet of the animal to the hooks on the end of the single tree, it was hoisted up to the scaffold, using the rope and pulley. The blood was drained into a tub, which was kept stirred from time to time, to prevent clotting so it could be used for one of the traditional products that people of this culture used to enjoy.

The belly was then slit from the upended bottom to the neck, and the heart, liver and other useful organs were removed to a waiting tub, with the rest of the intestines set aside.

The carcass was then lowered into the barrel of scalding hot water, and the boilers were returned to the cook stove to again be available as the work progressed.

The scalded hog was raised out of the steaming barrel; and Clarence, his father, and another neighbor swiftly scraped the bristles, which had been loosened by the scalding, from the skin The pig's head was sawed off and put in a tub to be taken to the house for Ida to continue preparing it to be used as head cheese, a meat that would later be sliced for sandwiches, etc. By this time the blood was cooled enough that the tub could be set on ice that had been brought from the local ice house.

Remembering past incidents of over-lifting when in a delicate condition, Ida stepped aside and let Clarence's dad carry the hefty tub with the hog's head into the house and onto the kitchen work table. Ida, who viewed this job as a reprieve from the more bloody and strong-smelling area of the butchering, finished scraping and cleaning the head. What a scene it was, eighteen-month-old Dane dancing around in excitement and gingerly touching the pig's head in curiosity and baby Jimmy babbling and flopping his chubby hand from his perch on Gerena's lap.

Finally, when all was cleaned up, edible organs in their containers, and the cleaned head sitting on the table, Ida sat back with a sigh. Enduring her nausea while doing all these things left her weary. As she looked around the room before launching into the next round of pork-related tasks, she noticed that the mouth of the cleaned-up head on the table seemed to be formed into an amusing grin. She reflected on the ready grin of her neighbor, Sal, and thought with amusement and a twinge of guilt, "Doesn't that look a little like Sal's grin?" Pushing the thought quickly from her mind, Ida set out morning coffee and freshly-baked treats for the men.

Before the men showed up at the door, Sal knocked her special knock and popped in. Finished with her own morning chores and ready to help as she had promised, Sal had picked up little Lawrence and had come across the road to pitch in. Examining the prepared head on the work table, Sal remarked, in her hearty way, "My, doesn't its smile look like me?" Ida could have fainted. Could her thoughts have been read? She would never know, because she wasn't about to share, "That's exactly what I was thinking!"

Though Ida kept her thoughts securely concealed for the time being, a priceless memory and teaching opportunity came out of the incident. Years later she shared the story with her young daughter, and together they laughed as Ida intimated that the amusing thoughts in our minds are not always the ones we can share.

The rest of the meat processing went as ordered, according to family tastes and facilities: hams and sides of bacon were taken to Grandpa Hanson's smokehouse; and feet, joints, and ears were put into brine for pickling. The head was cooked and the meat removed and pressed in a cheesecloth bag and placed in brine for the head cheese. Most of the organ meat was prepared and eaten the first few days. Chops and other cuts were packed in salt to preserve them and were stored in stoneware crocks. The fat was trimmed off the meat and the internal fat was ground in the cast iron meat grinder and heated in the woodstove oven to melt off the fat that would be saved for baking.

The extra hands were priceless, and the help would certainly be returned in kind when the Ericksons were ready to butcher. And, while many pigs would be butchered on the Watrud farm through the years, none would have such a surprising and amusing sidelight as this one that resembled Sal's smile.

10 New Horizons

See the loom
with the weaver from above.
Tangled threads underneath
show order and love.

Another autumn signed on, showing its hint in red edges on the maples, browning of the corn tassels, and drying of the husks on the earliest planted corn. Clarence's shifts at the canning factory became fewer as cutting and shocking the ripe corn, as well as cutting and chopping corn for the silo filled much of the time he wasn't milking or feeding cows. Little Jimmy was creeping and pulling himself up on anything available while Dane egged him on. Teens that had helped off and on during haying time were back in school.

Ida was still the husking champion, as the picked corn was brought into the shed. This job came after she had taken her turn picking and tossing corn into the wagons. These wagons were equipped for the corn picking, with one side built up with boards to stop the corn that was picked and thrown into the wagon from falling over the other side.

This only worked for corn picked before being cut, but depending on how dry the ripe corn was, some of it could be husked as it was picked. It meant that available help could be used while weather was favorable.

Soon the frost made it necessary to can the last of the tomatoes from the garden and carry the squash, pumpkins, and potatoes to the root cellar for storage. Peas, beans, corn, and carrots had been canned in jars during the summer; everything was ready for family meals through the winter.

With the invigorating freshness of the fall air after the heat and humidity of summer and so many seasonal tasks completed, the daily chores, care of the babies, and laundry seemed a light load to Ida. Her thoughts turned to Thanksgiving and Christmas preparations. Many gifts were already laid up in the form of various family members' favorite special jams and preserves, and again, the short span of evening between chores and bedtime would be spent knitting socks for Pa and Clarence and cuddly bed socks for Agnes, sewing a nightie for Ma, and making little things for the new addition on the way. She was tempted to sew ruffled bonnets and dresses, but caution told her there was plenty of time to start such gender specific garments when the wearer is known.

Another interest came into the mix. Always interested in new ideas and ways to make farm living more productive, Clarence had been talking with his cousin Beulah's new husband. Beulah's husband, active in agriculture research, was working with a new experiment station at Spooner, Wisconsin, toward the development of more productive hybrid seed.

Viewing this as a way to expand their farming operation, Clarence began studying ways to equip the farm to enable this new venture.

There were many steps on the way to becoming a producer of hybrid seed. A building built specifically for the purpose of enabling corn to be dried adequately to be used for seed was a necessity, and an improved barn was really needed before they would be ready to launch a new operation. Late fall cutting of trees that grew on the farm, in addition to firewood needed for winter heat and cooking, began to lay the groundwork for new buildings.

The snow came, and now the cattle were more confined in the barn. The manure that accumulated each day was hauled out on the bobsled, both adding fertilizer to the fields and keeping the barnyard clean. Snip and King were harnessed up each day for this job, and this kept them from getting lazy and soft. Bud, the new colt was growing fast and showed signs of becoming a big work horse. Clarence took Snip, the bronco mare, to the Percheron stud that had sired Bud.

Pa and Ma and Agnes came to the farm as much as possible before the really severe weather set in. Agnes was confined to a wheelchair as a result of rheumatoid arthritis that struck her as a teenager, and it was a real effort for her to go out. Ma also was hampered by arthritis, so visits with Pa, Ma, and Agnes were more often going "up home," (Ida's term for their home farm) than for Pa to bring Ma and Agnes.

The onset of Agnes's arthritis had been a bitter pill, as well as a painful disability for a young girl. Ida and Agnes were only about a year apart in age, and as they completed elementary school, Pa and Ma decided they could send only one of them to high school. This was because high school would involve the student living in a distant town and would require extra money for the additional expenses. Since Agnes was an exceptional student, Pa and Ma decided she would be the one to get a higher education. Although Ida would have loved to have gone to high school as well, she agreed to stay home and help Ma with the younger children.

Tragedy struck, as into her second year of high school, boarding with a family in Rice Lake, Wisconsin, Agnes was stricken with very severe rheumatoid arthritis. She was in such pain that even a touch was unbearable. Agnes' hope of education was dashed, and the family put forth every effort, traveling as needed, to find a cure. Ida was needed at home more than ever now—not only to care for the younger children, but to help care for her precious, close sister as well. In spite of her condition, Agnes had a cheerful disposition, and every visit from her was a privilege.

With the motivation of accumulating logs for the upcoming building, and all the branch wood being cut up for firewood, the woodpile rapidly increased. Ida's brothers Harold and Oscar had gotten married and moved to Minneapolis, so this Christmas was a big home-coming gathering. The younger brother Carl had opted to stay and operate the farm with Pa. The gathering was an occasion for two-man crosscut saws to be used for a few days, and more hope of some building to happen by summer.

Ida's youngest sister Edna was in her last year of high school this Christmas, and her young boyfriend from the Russian community was included in their Christmas celebration, prompting the Hansons to extend their Christmas celebration on to the seventh of January, the Russian Christmas.

An older brother Helmer from Stone Lake, Wisconsin and his family joined in the celebration, and provisions for overnights were made by the local families, making the travel feasible and prolonging the activities.

Only Helmer and Ida had children at this point, and those children were the center of attention, making this Christmas celebration a foretaste of the huge festive gatherings of later years. Lefse, lutefisk, wonderful Swedish meatballs, roasted chicken and venison, followed by Ma's special green tomato mincemeat and apple and pumpkin pies, made up the biggest part of the meal. All the ladies provided Christmas cookies and special baked Scandinavian delicacies.

"Well, Ida," Pa said, in a rare private moment, "is your new baby going to be a husky one like the two you have?" Knowing her longing for a girl, he gave her a little nudge and a kiss on the forehead, his generously wide mustache tickling her. His empathy was conveyed as he looked into her eyes and nodded his affirmation that she would do fine, adding the words, "You always come through."

Pa fingered the deerskin scroll she had given him, printed in her fine quill script, "My beloved Father," and the treasures of being Pa's 'little shadow' were momentarily relived in two minds.

11 Snowballing Family

The months roll by, and busy days
leave hardly time to daydream on.
A heart prepared to thank and praise,
finds warm fulfillment in each dawn.

The days, which were taken up with bearing up against the cold, shoveling the ever-gathering snow to facilitate the moving of cattle, feeding livestock, and milking cows gradually began to grow longer. The lamplight glowed on Clarence's paper as he continued to map out his ever-progressing plans for his hopes: a sound dairy barn, a corn house to house his seed production venture, a farm business to support his wife, sons, and the new child soon to come.

February, the month the baby was due, was just around the corner. "This time we'll make sure the doctor is on hand, even if we have to keep him at the house!" Clarence joked. But beneath his quick humor, he was anxious to reassure Ida, who so often had to bear the risks and inconvenience. Christine and one of the older cousins came to help a few days early, and along with Gerena, the three of them made the home happily sociable and well-prepared for the birth.

Early signs of labor began, and Clarence wasted no time driving to the Blairs to call the doctor, who arrived fairly early. It was fortunate he was there, as his presence spared Christine having to deal with minor complications that would have slowed down the delivery. Throughout the hours and efforts that ensued, Christine held onto fervent hope that this time her dear sister Ida would be able to use the ruffled bonnets.

"Wonderful news!" Dr. Nelson announced, holding up the squirming, crying infant. "Your two little blond boys have a healthy black-haired brother."

"Oh, thank God!" Ida said, smiling through tears, "We're naming him LeRoy. It means the king, you know; and that's what a new baby always is—first place in everyone's time. A prince at heart, but not a ruler." No one mentioned bonnets nor the name Lois; but the charm and cuteness of the new brother was heralded in abundance.

Clarence and Ida appreciated the regular February blessings—planting time still a few weeks off, but the hopefulness of spring mounting on those few rare days when the mercury climbed out of the cellar. Seed catalogs came in the mail; Ida started cabbage and tomato seeds in flats in the south windows, along with special flower seed saved from last year's blossoms as well as from friends.

Dane's increasing vocabulary brought frequent smiles, as he began calling himself Ding a Bob—his construction of "Dane Robert." He also called Jimmy "Boy," and Laddie's name was Bow Wow.

But even with all his cute phrases, Dane wasn't the least receptive to potty training, and Ida now had three sets of diapers to daily rinse and scrub on the washboard. On a visit during this time, Christine, ire welled up inside her, remarked to Clarence, "Isn't this a little much for Ida?" Clarence's withering expression was met with Christine's, "A good mother makes a good wife."

The snow melted in March's sunshine and grass began to edge the path and the yard, bringing a pleasant surprise. As he had followed Lawrence and the other boys around outside, Dane observed something that didn't happen when they were cooped up in the house during the winter. With his newly increased vocabulary, Dane asked cheerfully, "Shall I go pee-pee on the grass?" The diaper laundry dwindled a little, along with a growing helpfulness, growing golden curls that Ida couldn't bear to cut, and lots of baby talk from little Jimmy, who had a mop of flaxen waves, also off limits for the shears.

Dark-haired baby LeRoy was a contrast to his brothers, both in coloring and in his quiet, bashful charm. Still, a hint of strong will evidenced, much to the delight of the family, who had guessed that his quiet ways might indicate passiveness. They first noticed this strong will as he resisted the fastening of a cute aviator-style cap (the alternative to the not-mentioned bonnet) with a set expression and rigid bearing.

By fall, LeRoy was almost independently mobile, and the children became "the three boys," by which they were known in the family through their growing-up years. Seasonal planting and reaping came and went like clockwork, with neighbors and families growing closer or discussing different points of view. In Clarence, they had a lively and witty neighbor to debate and with whom to laugh. The pile of logs for building mounted by degrees, as did Clarence's paperwork and communication, along with viewing of operations that were in initial stages of operation for producing hybrid seed.

Threshing was a very busy time, both social and strenuous. Many neighbors, after the individual cutting and shocking of the oats from each farm, would gather and make use of the threshing machine (owned by a local farmer or implement dealer) which separated the feed grain from the straw which would be used as livestock bedding.

Everyone referred to this as the "threshing run," and the farmers who were in the group would bring their teams of horses and wagons and gather up the oat shocks from the fields and hoist them into the threshing machine. The machine would blow a steady stream of straw onto a pile in a designated place, forming a high shimmering golden dome, usually supported to keep it erect by an expertly placed stacking pole. At the same time, the oats grain would emerge from a spout on the machine to be caught in bags by some of the farmers, who would then carry the bags to a bin in the granary or barn and return to refill them and repeat the process.

Each farmer's wife had her work cut out for her. When her family's turn in the threshing came, she would need to be prepared to feed the men from seven or eight farms for two to four meals. The families who farmed more acres of oats needed to provide more meals, as more hours were required to thresh those oats.

Ida was again thankful for friends and family at these times. With two toddlers and a baby along with steady preparation, cooking on the wood stove, and serving, elderly Gerena wasn't a match for the activity that exceeded Ida's time and hands. Sal, one of the other neighbors, or one of Ida's sisters would come over and visit, enjoy the boys, and help with the stream of serving.

During a neighboring family's threshing turn, a not-so-amusing-at-the-time incident occurred at the end of one of those hard earned meals. The wife, after serving her huge meal, stepped out of the pantry with a pie in her hand. "Nobody wants pie," she announced, and she returned it to the pantry. Startled threshers remembered the incident unfavorably for years.

The garden, increased in size with more mouths to feed, and the canning and preserving were well on their way to being wound up for the season; and now the harvesting of the corn was at hand. Clarence was dreaming that perhaps this would be the last year—or nearly so—that the corn would be merely a feed crop, but that it soon would be the source of extra income as certified seed corn.

Steers and hogs were again butchered cooperatively with neighbors, and Pa's and Uncle Hjalmer's smoke houses were packed with hams, bacon, and sausage, and later in the fall, venison. Pa was beginning to be called "Grandpa" more often, with toddler boys talking to him and the Stone Lake Hanson family of older children being on hand at least two or three times a year.

Another big Hanson Christmas rolled around with all its traditional cooking and getting better acquainted with new in-laws. The Clear Lake farm felt like it would be their home for a lifetime, and it was a joy to spend time with friends coming and going with special baked goods and sometimes just coffee.

The Grandpa and Grandma Watrud Christmas was less structured, with Clarence and Ida always spending a day around Christmas at his sister Adeline and her husband Oscar's home, enjoying their young adult twins, two teen-age daughters, and two more sons. Clarence had worked on their farm some before marrying Ida, and there was a special bond there. Or they would go to his brother Lester's on the Rice Lake farm where Clarence and Ida had started farming. Joe and Belle had moved to an adjoining farm, so the visit to the senior Watruds would usually include them all. An older brother, Morris, was operating a restaurant at Spooner, Wisconsin, and another brother, Martin, was in the merchant marines. Clarence's youngest brother was also now trying his hand at the restaurant business. Second-oldest sister, Charlotte, lived in Michigan with her family, and their visits took place in the summer; but it was fun to send out and look forward to receiving Christmas packages in the mail.

At home, ladies' aid meetings became central to Ida's social life, along with services at the beautiful Moe church. Clarence now found himself accompanied during barn chores by an eager helper—a wiry two-and-a-half-year-old Dane. "Be careful with the fork….Don't try to carry everything at once," were common reminders during this time. Little "Granddad" Jimmy was fast on his big brother's heels, making it an extra effort until order was established to keep the "I help" eagerness in safe limits.

12 Babe and New Horizons

The bridge is out; the road is mire,
and the creamery is five miles away.
Full milk cans, need for help is dire.
New barn timbers' forfeit save the day.

Ida's gift for a poetic slant on situations, which she seldom had time for these busy days, focused on the current predicament: the bridge was out. As spring arrived, days and weeks seemed imperative as progress toward the hoped-for new farming venture—raising seed corn—encountered many roadblocks. Along with time constraints and material and cash limitations, this one more complication was a severe setback. Taking from the slowly amassing log pile to rebuild the bridge across the little creek that crossed the driveway seemed out of proportion with the size of the goals Clarence had in mind. Patience and prayer were the order of the day, as Clarence swallowed hard to the realization that it would now be at least another year before he could grow and process the corn.

His hope had been that once the soil dried enough, planting could be completed. When the busiest shifts at the canning factory tapered off, work to get logs sawed into lumber and constructing foundations for the new buildings could begin.

With help from neighbors, the logs were assembled and built into an adequate bridge, and the milk could again be taken to market. Although no one wanted to complain, it was still difficult not to note that flooding of this magnitude took place only once in a decade or so, and it would have to come when the materials and time were so precious.

A bright spot in the midst of it all came when Clarence went to harness the horses to pull the cart of milk cans out to the road, where one of the neighbors who had their pickup out could take them on to the creamery. Snip, the bronco mare that was part of his team proudly stood there with a wobbly midnight brown foal. "Well, a filly!" Clarence exclaimed, "Should make a good teammate for Bud." Bud was now almost two and would soon be ready to be ground driven alongside King to be trained as a workhorse. Clarence chuckled ironically, "Another development to help us learn patience."

Ida was thrilled. An animal lover, she immediately patted the damp and wobbly foal. "You'll be Babe, a partner for Bud, and you'll be a wonderful team." So, this once, Snip missed the daily chore of hauling the milk cans to the road. Fortunately, the Ericksons had hauled their milk cans out and had their wagon ready. With a new bridge, and having accepted the slight reduction of the log pile, a new spring underway didn't look so bad.

Family and community life had changed in the passing years at the rural East Clear Lake home, now three little boys instead of two babies. Young children playing together when the farmers and their wives would visit, a comradeship was born of knowing the virtues as well as quirks of one another. Talk turned to the local school, as some of the families had school age children or grandchildren. Ida pictured the two and a half mile distance for her little boys a few short years down the road, and she wondered if she would get around to learning to drive the car as her oldest and youngest sister did, but that was for another day.

As the growing season came and went, it was brightened by the company of nephew Bob Yoss, Charlotte and Fred's son, who came to help with haying and cultivating corn. His extra hands to help with milking cows were a blessing too. And with Laddie now trained to get the cows alone when Clarence called for them, Clarence was all around freed with more time to cut wood for building materials and stove wood.

Peaceful years passed as the boys grew, groundwork was laid for the future, and weddings among both Ida and Clarence's relatives increased the extended family. A beloved family picture froze in time the young father, soft and loving mother, two blond little boys who looked like little girls in their long ringlets and shining, flaxen waves, and the youngest boy with his soft dark hair and the cutest baby smile. Not apparent on this picture, deep beneath the mother's heart, was a little girl. Only Clarence and Ida knew of the presence, but not the gender.

The following year the picture was much different. That little formal portrait was the goodbye to those long, blond curls, but little did they know, a forerunner to other blond curls. This Christmas Uncle Hjalmer played Santa Claus at the Hanson gathering, and four-year-old Dane fairly trembled with excitement as he approached him, while three-year-old Jimmy said soberly, "Hi, Unca' Hjalmer." LeRoy's response was never relayed, probably a bashful smile. Gifts at this time were mainly necessities, but, usually a toy for each.

Winter rolled on, with a surprising break in the weather early in March. The snow thawed, and it became warm enough that Ida planted a few flowers, tucking straw over them at night to keep them warm. It was time for the new baby, and every preparation was in place. The boys were tucked in for the night, and Ida and Clarence sat up by lamplight for a little while. "It's probably nothing," Ida remarked, "but I feel a little twinge." Suddenly they heard a crash of thunder, and rain began beating on the roof. Clarence pulled on his oilskin coat and went out and started the pickup to get Christine. On the way, he stopped at the Blair's house and called the doctor. Dr. Nelson was out on an emergency and couldn't be reached. The rain quickly turned to a heavy, wet snow, and Clarence was glad just to be able to maneuver the old Dodge pickup to Christine and Hjalmer's.

Hjalmer said he needed to stay at home to do his own chores, in case the roads became impassable; so he sent Christine on with Clarence. They slewed and prayed as they headed for the Watrud farm. It may be that it wasn't time yet, because Ida usually had gotten in a more intense labor early in the process.

However, it was urgent for her to have good care in attendance. Gerena would have been helpless if labor progressed.

They pulled into the yard, already deep with snow, and Christine slid out and hurried through the slushy snow to the house. Gerena announced as she greeted her at the door, "Ida had to lie down. Her pains are coming fast." Clarence was thankful he had taken the precaution of asking the Blairs to continue trying to reach Dr. Nelson, because getting in and out of their driveway could have lost too much time, or they could have been stuck

Christine, bless her efficiency, arranged all the sterile sheets and cloths that Ida had prepared and provided water and cheerful company. Everyone settled into the unpredictable wait for the doctor. The wait was shortened beyond any human power to extend it. Ida tried to wait, then needed to relax, and nature took over. A mighty thrust brought the new infant into Christine's waiting hands, free from any impediment, and she held up the tiny—girl! Ida, above her exhaustion, laughed and cried all at once. "And she's healthy. Oh I'm so blessed. Clarence, she can be named for you—Carol—a song of joy."

Well, Christine wasn't supposed to be midwife this time, but you know who puts things in order. Bless her heart. What a sister! All this had taken place between bedtime and 1:15 a.m. There was still time for a little sleep after the baby and mother were cleaned up and situated. Clarence had really risen to the occasion and done his part, and, even though it was a family joke that he could certainly sleep, no one begrudged it.

As you might guess, although the adults at the Watrud home hadn't gotten much sleep, three little boys were wide awake before daylight, bounding into Ida's room unimpeded. The new baby was bundled in the bassinet, right up against the bed. Dane and Jimmy peeked over the edge. "It's little," Dane whispered. Ida sat up just in time to see Dane and Jimmy attempting to hoist LeRoy up to see the new baby. She reached out her arm and slid the covering from the baby's face as Christine, alerted by the lively entrance of the boys, came and lifted LeRoy up to see little Carol. One of his memorable early phrases was chirped as he viewed her, "So sveet an' coot." What an endorsement!

As the pale daylight dawned, the clank of harness buckles and chains could be heard as Clarence drove Snip and King out to the road to pull Hjalmer's car into the yard through the drifts and mud. Hjalmer had, on his way to the Watrud farm to hear the news, picked up one of the nieces to help Ida so he could take Christine back home to help him. Uncle Hjalmer also brought sad news: The emergency that had kept Dr. Nelson away was the emergency delivery of a stillborn baby girl on the other side of Clear Lake. Another family was as filled with grief as the Watruds were filled with joy.

Little pink dresses, booties, and bonnets bedecked the little dresser Clarence had fashioned from fruit crates and Ida had covered with ruffled white chintz. She had taken pains to avoid girl colors until she knew if the new baby would be a girl or boy. Moe Church buzzed with news of the new arrival, and Ida and Clarence's families showered baby Carol with attention.

One of the elderly church ladies commented, seeing her in a little blue-flowered dress, "Little blue Yay."

More exciting news came in just three days. Clarence's sister Adeline also had a baby girl, so there were two tiny girl cousins—Carol a little wispy-haired blond, and Loretta, a rosy brunette. As soon as the two families were able to get together, the two baby girls were baptized on the same day, in the same fount.

This was the year for sharing news of family additions. Sal and Lars were soon blessed with a new baby son, and Ida had opportunities to return some of the child care favors Sal had done for her. Their new little boy was named Samuel, and "Sammy" became a playmate to Carol when they were old enough to get around. The Pearsons, another neighbor family, had a new daughter they named Ann, who became company for her brother Lennie. Get-togethers now were a sharing of child care topics and exchanged care while doing errands. Ladies aid bubbled with little ones, getting settled, being held. It was often sewing circle, but this fell a little more to the mothers of older children and grandmothers.

Less than two weeks after Carol's birth, the family was hit with scarlet fever and had to be quarantined for ten days or until the doctor declared them free of the illness. Chores had to be done in special clothes that weren't worn in the house, and those doing the milking or handling the milk had to wear masks. Ida never knew for sure if baby Carol contracted scarlet fever or not.

There was just a little rash and peeling that could have been normal infant rash. The little boys got very sick. Dane relinquished his "right-hand-helper" role, and Jimmy announced, "I'm not Granddad; I'm just a sick little boy."

Little two-year-old LeRoy began to show a new side of his personality. Always quite smiley and agreeable, with only short-lived displays of determination, he began to surprise Ida and Clarence a little as his speaking progressed. Once, after watching his brothers, arguing a little over processes, build towers with blocks, LeRoy quietly pushed the bottom block, causing a collapse. "I make it vorse." he quietly said under his breath. The halo slipped a little, but LeRoy was still a pretty good little boy.

This was also the year for the building of the new barn. Clarence planned it with a foundation of vertical logs, with a gambrel roof above the haymow to allow for ample hay storage. The timing was good, because the old barn was sagging almost to caving in, and the roof had deteriorated to the point that the wooden shingles were a mass of sodden slivers and the eaves almost touched the ground. Dane and Jimmy, now three and four, and very resourceful at finding recreation, saw the sagging, low profile roof as a perfect slide and enthusiastically put it to use. They soon rued their wonderful choice of fun, as they cried with their little behinds full of splinters. Ida, Clarence, and Gerena did their best to remove them as mercifully as possible. So, no one was disappointed to see that old building come down, and there was a bonus: it provided kindling to start fires in the wood stoves for several years.

The long hoped-for corn house was now begun, with plans for drying bins and shelling and grading areas being perfected. Ida even designed a "Watrud Wisconsin Seed Corn emblem" for the corn sacks. With excitement, Clarence ordered from the agriculture experiment station the precious seed combination necessary to produce a hybrid, to be delivered when the equipment was ready for production.

Bob Yoss came again from Michigan to help with building and with the farm work during the busy planting and haying season. Clarence's dad, who had a lot of knowledge of building, was able to be free some of the time to advise and help. Relatives and friends who had older children assured Clarence that when the time came to put the seed corn plans into action, there would be help for the exacting job of detasseling the corn that was not to be pollinating parent corn. So, the summer and winter, along with the work of each season moved on, and changes came about on the Watrud farm.

Household chores on the farm were without much in the way of convenience, with the laundry scrubbed on ribbed washboards in galvanized wash tubs and the water heated in copper boilers on the wood cook stove. This summer Ida was pleased that they were able to get a wringer that could attach to one of the washtubs, and by turning a crank, much of the water could be wrung out of the washed clothes. Entertaining the three boys with conversation and singing, Ida felt the job was moving right along. Suddenly a piercing scream came from one of the boys.

Curious about how those gears could get the rollers to wring out the clothes, in an instant when no one was looking, Jimmy stuck his hand between the gears, catching his little finger. Fortunately Clarence was nearby to help Ida free him from the wringer. Jimmy's little finger hung loose, held only by a strip of skin. They immediately loaded all the boys into the old pickup and hurried to Clear Lake, where Dr. Nelson expertly sewed the little finger back on. "I make no guarantees," he said, "but I congratulate you two on your quick action. I hope you'll soon find this little guy's finger as good as new."

Time passed, and Jimmy's finger healed and became useful again. Not to be outdone, with summer not yet past, Dane was the victim of another laundry incident. Watching the laundry process from the porch rail, he fell and landed on the rim of the washtub. His lower cheek was cut clear through, releasing a mouthful of Aunt Christine's good oatmeal cookie. Dr. Nelson quipped that his sewing practice was certainly encouraged by the Watrud boys.

In the wintertime, the washtubs were brought into the kitchen, both for the family laundry and for weekly baths. Set near the pot-bellied heater and filled with warm water, the tubs served their purpose well. There was an amusing incident when Gerena accidentally came through the kitchen door while Clarence was bathing. Although she quickly covered her eyes and backed out, those rascally little boys claimed that she peeked between her fingers.

13 Sunnyside

Two and a half miles
for two little boys,
facing the world
with its troubles and joys.

Summer again drew reluctantly to a close. Bob Yoss headed home to Michigan, and the teens who had helped during haying and harvest no longer sat at the Watrud dinner table or under the elms for lemonade at afternoon break.

For one Watrud boy, summer's close couldn't come too soon. Dane had been told he could start school in the first grade in the fall, even though he would not be six until October first. He gleefully packed and unpacked the prized lunch box that had been bought for him and joined the neighbor boys who would be starting school with him.

This joining with the neighbor children was the most fun part for the younger Watrud children, as they got to know Norman and Lula Hummel, Lenny and Ann Pearson, and the Mitchell children, who were a little older. Since LeRoy was one of the "three boys," he was allowed to join in. Little Carol, who was walking now, had displaced Dane as the one with the head of golden curls and was often the center of attention, being shown off by older brothers when the friends got together.

Sunnyside School, the one-room, eight-grade school the children were to attend, was two and a half miles from home. Ida wondered about the feasibility of her five-year-old making the trip, but Lawrence Erickson was an upper-grader, and it was decided that Dane would start out the hike to school with him, joining the others on the way.

The house was alive with excitement, and likely a few tears as well, as Ida saw her first child off down the driveway. They all watched as Dane started out with his special lunch box and school supplies. Sadly, before the school year was over, that precious lunch box was abused by an older bully, which resulted in Dane wielding a baseball bat and sullying his sweet image.

Each Christmas season, the classroom would become a theater, and the little school children would learn their pieces to recite or their parts for the school play and present them to the parents and relatives. These events were huge for the preschool members of the families, as it was their opportunity to run in the playroom with "big" kids following the program and to have special goodies brought by "Santa Claus."

Moe Church also was a wonderland for very little ones, with lights festooned with garlands and candles, flanked by holly and balsam. A second Christmas treat of candy and nuts, and usually a big red apple, would be distributed to eager, giggling or shyly smiling boys and girls; and then off to Grandma's or Auntie's for more festivities.

To this day, ladies in their nineties sometimes tell Carol they remember her at those festivities with her three brothers and her blond curls. The school programs and church socials were a wonderful way for children to learn to appreciate their neighbors and bask in the loving fellowship of such a sacred and joyful season.

The school year ended with the school picnic, again with the opportunity for the littler Watruds to play with big kids. Carol delighted in having Lula and the other little girls walk her around, carefully pushing swings, and watching her brothers footrace and play wheelbarrow and other playground games. It was a thrill to her to be included in eating a shared dinner from the different families that came. Jimmy, too, was in his glory, knowing he would be starting first grade the following year.

By the time Jimmy started school at Sunnyside, the Watruds' place in the little school had been established. Still, beginners always have to meet the test, and jacket or baseball—whatever was Jimmy's special possession was challenged by the older bully-types. Thankfully, Mrs. Timm ran a pretty tight ship and expected fair treatment for all.

LeRoy grew up a lot that fall, with both older boys gone at school. He and Carol were playmates, and he was always on hand to watch after Carol as the two of them followed Mama and Daddy around doing chores. When Gerena felt up to keeping Carol in the house, LeRoy was Clarence's helper.

Then, there were the school programs with opportunities to play with other kids. When the older boys could include LeRoy in their fun, he was in his glory. And little Carol enjoyed the school girls, who were always excited to entertain her, brushing her curls or lugging her around.

The walks to ladies' aid with Mama were a delight. Carol was always fascinated by the handwork the women created. Then, also, she enjoyed the wide array of ladies willing to respond to her "whys." Ida probably appreciated it every bit as much as Carol, because mamas do like to talk to grownups when they get a chance.

One walk to ladies aid at Mabel Blair's house was especially memorable to Carol. Before they left home, she had gotten in the way and knocked the heavy flat iron down onto her foot. While the injury was probably pretty minor, Carol didn't object to being carried all the way to the meeting or to being fussed over by the ladies.

14 Soaking Up a Summer

A little piece of heaven,
that Clear Lake farm place,
held in loving regard
as new days we face.

  The summer before LeRoy started the first grade had to be the most memorable one at the Clear Lake farm. The new barn was finished and in use. The corn house, with its slatted bins for drying corn, had been erected and stood in its place between house and barn. Clarence had actually planted his first crop of hybrid seed corn, and the Department of Agriculture came out to the farm for regular inspections.

Teen age nieces and nephews were hired for the upcoming job of detasseling as the corn matured. Out of every eight rows of corn, only two rows—the ones that carried the gene of the variety of corn that would fertilize the seed to form the hybrid—would keep their tassels, because it was through the tassels that pollination would take place. The other six rows had to have the tassels thoroughly removed to prevent those plants from producing pollen. This necessity turned out to be a great delight to Carol, as the company of these young people, along with cousin Bob who helped with haying in the summer, brought a lot of pleasure to the little girl.

Across the road, at that little farm, Sammy and his mother, Sal,
what a delight for a little girl to have a neighbor pal.
Nurtured on that rocky farm, though at length, she moved away,
she missed going to play with Sammy and when Sammy came to play.
Carol was three years old that spring, and Clarence and Ida decided she could cross the road to play with Sammy Erickson if someone was watching her.

The Ericksons had a pair of guinea fowl, whose screeching and squawking alerted the family to approaching visitors, much the same as the barking of a watchdog does. The guineas were fascinating to Carol and Sammy, as they looked a bit like small turkeys and side-stepped briskly to avoid little hands that might interfere with them.

One chilly April day, Carol wore her warm bright red mittens when she went to play at Sammy's. At noon she went home for lunch, and as she chatted with Mama about the fun things they had done, she realized her mittens were missing. Daddy and Mama helped her look for them for a while, and Carol suddenly remembered the guineas. "The guineas must have eaten them!" she exclaimed. Mama prayed with her that the mittens would show up, but Carol was quite sure they wouldn't be found, because the guineas had surely eaten them.

Being only three, Carol was still young enough for a nap. Her naptime must have been a welcome relief to the rest of the household who had listened to lengthy testimony of her conviction that the guineas had eaten her mittens. After her nap, as Carol enjoyed her usual snack and glass of milk, she suddenly noticed her mittens on the sewing machine by the door. She was very embarrassed that she had been so wrong and looked from face to face to make sure no one was laughing at her.

Even before the corn was planted, with the anticipated extra help for detasseling not yet in the picture, cousin Bob Yoss came to help prepare fields and plant crops.

Carol was given the privilege of carrying a little container of water or a snack to the workers in the field when they were working close enough that she could remain in view of the house. It could be a lovely little walk if it were in the part of the field near the small creek. She would see the blue flag iris and duck weed, and sometimes dragonflies; maybe even a frog if she was lucky.

One day, when she had ambled across the dusty field to Bob, he kidded, "You took good care of my water now, didn't you?" Perhaps catching the jesting tone, she answered, "Well, a frog jumped in, but I took him out." Her imagination was the source of laughter for quite a while.

That June brought about a diversion in the general routine of farming. As Clarence was in the field mowing hay with the horse-drawn mower, the steady "snick-snick" of the mower blades faltered as a sudden shower of feathers flew from the rapidly reciprocating sickle.

With apprehension of breakdown and lost time, Clarence reined in Bud and Babe, the team of horses that had now settled into being dependable and steady. He wrapped the driving line on the mower lever and stepped down to see what blocked the mower's progress. There the brave bundle of feathers lay mangled in strands of freshly cut hay. "It could be the mother of some pheasant chicks," he reasoned. "Nothing but danger to her chicks would have driven her to sit still through her own peril."

He searched until he found a nest of speckled eggs nearby in a finely coiled nest of grass. "I wonder...," Clarence said to himself as he gently gathered the eggs into his chore coat. He raised the mower sickle and turned the horses, along with the tiny cargo, back toward the barn where a "clucky" hen back in the chicken house was sitting on eggs. Just maybe, she would hatch these pheasants along with her chicks.

The protective clucky hen ruffled wings and feathers and made threatening sounds as Clarence invaded her nest—her stronghold on the farm—with his hand. He gently slipped the tiny eggs beneath her warm wings. One, two, three, four, five, six, beside her five or six chicken eggs many times their size. "Chicken eggs take twenty-one days to hatch," he thought. "Could the timing of these tiny interlopers possibly synchronize?"

That task finished, he went back out to the field and continued mowing hay. Days settled back to routine with milking cows, feeding pigs and chickens, and making hay. The first crop hay had been cut, raked, hauled and stored away, and no one had yet dared peek at the awaited eggs, but the day was nearing now.

And, sure enough, that feisty hen began
to fluff her feathery wings,
and look beneath and fluff again;
at last, stepped out with tiny little things.
Little puffballs, yellow and brown,
some walnut-sized, some size of hen's eggs,
all covered with soft, fluffy down,
scampering on tiny legs.

That little hen was a model mother, scratching up seeds and grain for the tiny pheasants with no less care than she gave her own chicken babies. It was comical to watch the tiny legs of the mini-sized chicks scamper to keep up with the regular chicks.

Summer days marched on, with the busyness of farm life. Chicks feathered out and tried their wings. The tiny pheasants startled the others by leaving the ground a bit, while the regular chicks were earth bound. The poultry house continued to be their home, and, although the young pheasants had the ability of wild birds, their bonding with their domestic siblings kept them from venturing out to a life in the wild.

15 Storm Clouds and Shivarees

Grown boys and girls at work and play;
some must give up the hand they hold.
Dads and moms see their sons go away;
display blue stars—some, sadly, gold.

Summer passed, with at least as much excitement as Carol anticipated. The nieces and nephews who were hired for the corn detasseling were tolerant of her teasing and questions, while Ida often diverted her attention other directions to enable workers to work.

Clarence also hired extra help during haying season, and this brought with it the new dimension of very interesting romantic intrigue. Walt, a young man of eighteen, and Dorothy, just fifteen years old, were hired to finish out the summer when the crew of cornfield workers finished up their work of the three or four week season. Dorothy helped Ida can fruit and vegetables for the winter. As Clarence was busy setting up and overseeing the drying and processing of the corn to ensure it met the state agricultural department standards, Walt worked with the dairy cows—not only milking them himself, but supervising Dane and Jimmy in learning to milk by hand. It was fun to watch the barn cats sit on their hind legs to have milk squirted into their mouths.

There had always been a bit of flirting among the teens who had detasseled corn; but Walt and Dorothy's relationship seemed different. They continued their interest in one another through the fall.

Jimmy and Dane were again walking the two and a half miles to school morning and night. When Carol wasn't off playing with Sammy, and when Leroy wasn't off doing a job for Clarence that Carol was too little to do, Carol pretty much had LeRoy to herself as a playmate. Meanwhile, Clarence and Ida would talk about the ominous news coming over the radio, and later, the alarming news of the attack on Pearl Harbor.

Carol kept lasting impressions of the war in her mind. She still vividly remembers her older cousin, Howard, coming to visit in his sailor uniform before he headed overseas.

She can still almost hear the reports of the young men who had been working on the farms in the area being drafted into service. Then, there is the memory of the grade school children taking part in scrap drives, gathering tin cans and metal to be remanufactured to help the war effort.

Christmas preparations went on as usual, but the big Hanson gathering would be short more than one of the young cousins, away in military training. That year LeRoy and Carol got realistic metal toy telephones that were their pride and joy, and many imaginative conversations went on over those make believe lines. "You got Prince Albert in the can? For goodness' sake, let him out!" LeRoy would say, and they would giggle endlessly. A lot of nonsense passed on those little toy phones.

Bud and Babe, the young horses Clarence was raising, were now trained well enough to pull the sleigh, and the children were diverted from the serious with a sleigh ride to Grandpa's to transport him to Aunt Christine's for the celebration. Grandma Hanson had passed away a year earlier, and Ida wanted to give her dad extra attention. Aunt Agnes, hampered by her arthritis, and Gerena rode with Aunt Edna and Uncle Pete in their car.

The talk at the gathering had heavy overtones with concerns about the war, now well underway. Soon after, though, the conversation turned to the upcoming wedding of Walt and Dorothy. Before the New Year was one week old, they were married by a judge and came back to live.

Carol and LeRoy were righteously indignant when Gerena banged their new phones together as percussion for a shivaree. The neighbors, though concerned over this very youthful marriage, were very enthusiastic in helping them launch their union with noisy glee.

As the winter progressed, other storm clouds seemed to be gathering around the Watrud farm. The credit that had facilitated the beginning of this hardworking operation tightened up, and as provisions were being made for another crop year, funds for the improvements and fuel and machinery to do more advanced farming were not as available as at the outset. Off and on, terms would come up in Clarence's and Ida's conversation about finance and Federal Land Bank. Carol and LeRoy thought that "Federal" guy must be kind of mean, and Clarence laughed wryly in response to their questions about Mr. Landbank.

The Norwegian Lutheran Church was the site of a heart wrenching scene that temporarily diminished the anxiety over the farm. A tiny girl, the daughter of Ida's distant cousin Cattie, ran up and down the wide entrance stairs crying, "They take our brothers and kill them!" Her mother caught her up in her arms, holding her close. That poor child's oldest brother was one of the first fatalities of the war. Ida cried with Cattie as she placed the gold star in the window. It had become the custom that parents of men who were serving in the United States military effort would place a blue star in their window. Should the son lose his life in service, it would be replaced with a gold star. This busy mother of seven children had become a Gold Star Mother.

Cousins Bob, Ken, and Carlyle enlisted, hoping for some chance of being placed in their chosen field. Talk came home from Sunnyside School of planting Victory Gardens to ease the demand for food, thus helping the war effort. Clarence remarked worriedly, "Our Victory Garden may have to be dug elsewhere."

The people from Federal Land Bank, who had financed the farming effort, were attempting to find another farm that possibly would require less financing. The expense of the crops that were not yet ready to sell had exhausted the available credit. The sturdy new barn, mostly hand built, and the beautiful made-to-order corn house, also built by hand, stood to be sadly deserted, as an unwanted move was to take place. That "Federal" guy seemed meaner than ever to LeRoy and Carol.

Mr. Van Sickle, the representative for the loan agency, announced to Clarence that he had located a farm that had been surrendered by its owners. "You can finance it with your equity in the Clear Lake farm," he suggested. Winter held its grip a few more months. Clarence and Ida looked at the prospective farm and spoke of it in low tones accompanied by serious expressions. Clarence, as ever, spoke about improvements that would make it livable and productive. Ida spoke little.

Sal and the other neighbor ladies gathered around, enjoying their remaining time with Ida and the children. Carol and Sammy plodded through the snow to cross the road and play together, little knowing their play-mate status would soon be past.

16 A Different Life

Into their lives, a ruler came,
lovely as she was severe.
A challenge to own and use and tame,
acres giving, though cost was dear.

As snow drifts began to settle in the warming sun and trickle into puddles and little icy streams on the gentle slopes of the yard, activity picked up on the Clear Lake farm. While Sammy and Carol played together, forming little rivulets by dragging small sticks through the slushy snow, the rest of the Watrud family gathered and packed the belongings worth keeping and moving from their six-year sojourn at the Clear Lake farm.

Four Year Old's Lesson:
When I was four, we moved today,
April first, long years away.
We moved with cows, pigs, chickens too,
even pheasants, home grown, a few,
to farm house on a hill so high
although weather beaten-- well, a sigh,
the view below, magnificent,
could have made us glad we went.

Why? to four-year-old not known.
The days were much like this same day,
not so many miles away.
patches of snow lingered below,
mud on boots and raw winds blow.
But, the scene when looking back,
reminds me, much I do not lack,
patched tarpaper torn and black
obstacles set Mama back:
How now to make a home?
Time has passed; I think that it was grit
that made them try and never quit.
that made me grow to search and see,
although sometimes, it sure was we
that got me perching higher up
someone beside me saying, "Yup.'
I could do it if I try,
or sometimes I just got by.
But I learned back at age four,
to give myself a better score,
when instead of just get by,
I'd try.

We scraped loose paint and calcimine,
we put the paving stones in line;
tore off loose siding, painted trim.

Daddy smiled when we helped him.
Held the boards while Grandpa nailed;
it seemed with help we really sailed.
When Mama painted one room blue
we all helped her paint another too.
The sighs that came from paint so chipped.
a four year old just laughed, and skipped.
and thought, "I helped a little bit."
That seemed to make the best of it.
and so as years and years go by,
I try.

"Daddy! Daddy! The pheasants are flying beside the truck."

Sure, enough. The entourage leaving the Clear Lake farm, healthy cattle driven along the shoulder of the road with older or weaker cattle aboard the truck, was suddenly flanked by half a dozen pheasants, flying and alighting by turns. The domestic chickens were in cages on the truck, and these pheasant offspring they had raised were not about to let them go.

Ida and four-year-old Carol rode in the truck with Clarence while brothers, eight-year-old Dane, seven-year-old Jimmy, and six-year-old LeRoy, plodded along behind and beside the walking cattle. Attempts to coax LeRoy into the truck had not been successful, as he wanted to be one of the "big boys," too. Young neighbor men had volunteered to help the boys herd the cattle along, and their company added a good deal of cheer and levity to the operation.

The new home awaited high on its hill above the large creek. Ida and the boys had already seen it, but to Carol, it was a new adventure. That's one of the perks of being four—what may be daunting hardships to those responsible, can seem like an adventure.

April first, traditional moving day for farmers, presented typical April weather. Patches of snow were still in various stages of melting. Mud was everywhere. Muddy ruts challenged the truck and plodding boots to travel the mile of makeshift driveway. Muddy county roads and muddy township roads funneled into the muddy driveway. Carol clapped and cheered over getting through each rut or mire.

Arriving at the turn into the farm, LeRoy finally gave in and allowed himself to be hoisted up into the cab of the truck. His overshoes were caked with inches of sticky mud, and his fatigue caused him to collapse on his mama and little sister.

Ida dispatched the offending mud with her deft, plump fingers, squeezing it off the sides and bottoms of each overshoe and snapping it to the ground with a flick of her wrist. The lighter weight feet scrunched up on Ida's aproned lap.

Clarence chuckled. "You probably won't want another turn at herding cows for a little while."

The large, faded red dairy barn dominated the yard as the truck strained into the yard. On, beyond the barn stood the tall, narrow, gambrel-roofed house, its narrow, weathered porch fastened flimsily to the south side. The siding was a faded grayish rust color, and the windows were, for a considerable part, covered with tar paper, some torn and curling away from the lath that held it. Ida looked only briefly and proceeded to unload the tired children that were clinging to her, survey where her help was needed in unloading, and trudged toward the shabby porch, nestling little shoulders with the free sides of her hands.

The help from the previous neighbors temporarily freed Ida so she could start a fire in the wood stove that had been just moved in. That stove with its door hanging unless propped, had been bought as a temporary fix until a better one could be found, and it became an ironic joke. The decision had presented itself often: Do we fix it or replace it? But it was still propped and moved right along with the family. A lot of delicious baked goods came from that old stove.

The fire started, Carol took her place on the temporary wood box to get warm by the stove. It may have been spring, but the ice tracing over the puddles as the sun lowered made it apparent that there was warming up to do. The coffee pot warmed on the stove, and LeRoy was directed to stay with Carol while Ida went to help settle the cows and the big bull into their new stalls.

Getting settled in the farmhouse was a family task. The fact that they had already moved the beds, dressers, and large oak kitchen dining table and chairs earlier made things a little easier now. They quickly set about covering the tears in the tar-paper covered windows.

The arrangement of the rooms was such that arranging furniture was done according to available space and immediate need, and the sequence of moving the remaining belongings and food went according to the arrangement. First, up five or six steps into the narrow porch, then through the front door, the only one on the main floor, into the large central room.

There was a brick chimney near the middle of the left side as you entered, to which were connected the heater stove on the far side and the cook stove on the near side. Clarence settled the cupboard he had hand built for their first home at Rice Lake onto a wall unhampered by windows. They arranged the table and chairs near that.

That, apparently, was the extent of accommodations for housekeeping. "But look!" Ida said, striving to lift her own spirits, "We have a pantry!" She was speaking of the tiny room to the side of the common room.

A small bedroom adequate for a double bed, dresser, and a curtained off corner for hanging space also brought her a sense of encouragement.

Up a narrow stairway was one large room with the chimney extending up through the center. The plan was to curtain off separate spaces for the boys and Carol. For now, boxes were stacked to make a temporary half-high partition.

"Yes, you will all put on pajamas and wash your hands and feet."

The cows assigned their stalls, milked by hand, and put into a temporary lot until the coming day's light would allow for a final check on the portion of the pasture that was fenced. Chickens were secured in the ramshackle brooder house, and the pigs were put into a small pig shelter under the trees. All this resulted in very tired boys and parents. Supper and sleep were at the fore of every mind.

"Now I lay me down to sleep…," drifted off on tired lips, and warm blankets on makeshift beds felt like Heaven.

17 The Morning After

April is here, and the earth is new;
the part that's winter is seeping away.
Overlook what is gone, find good in it too;
don't miss the sunshine by weeping today.

"It's okay to put your hands on the wall," Ida called as the children started down the stairs. Their Clear Lake home had had a hand rail, and there had been good reasons not to smudge the walls. But that wasn't the case yet, in this new house. Fixing up would come later; but for now, the priority was to get up and down the narrow, unstable stairs safely.

Carol slept until the sound of opening and closing doors awakened her. Then not to miss out on anything, she crept out of bed and peeped out of the upstairs window to see what it was like outside. It was still a half-snowy world with puddles interspersing lingering parts of drifts. Squirrels chattered in the trees west of the house, and sparrows pecked away among the dead stubble. A little pond seemed to be melting off among the trees. Mama had said yesterday that it must have been the old pigpen, and the little pond was a hog wallow.

People more responsible than little sleeping Carol had started the wood fire in the cook stove, and Ida's coffee wafted its fragrance through the house. Laddie was panting around the door, waiting to go out to the barn, He would have a new pasture to hunt for cows when the call, "Come, boss," sounded. And, what a pasture it was to be. The nearer part of the pasture, on the home side of the creek, dropped away down the tree-covered hill to flatten out near the creek. This lower part was still water-covered because of the flooding from melting snow. What couldn't be seen from the house was the continuation of the land along the creek to the west, steep hills appearing almost vertical.

Ida heated water on the cook stove. This would be used to wash cow udders before milking, as well to wash the milking equipment. Momentarily freed from directing children to start their chores, now waiting for corn bread to bake, she reflected, "Really, how will I cope with the change this time? The nearest neighbor is a mile away. Clarence said the phone line is not far away, and for the first time in our lives we can have a phone. I could call Edna and Christine. I think Sal and Mabel are long distance. That would mean emergency only. Oops! The corn bread is getting too brown."

So, tentative coping plans were set aside. The natural majesty of a tall, though neglected, home high on the hill softened a bit the lonely aspect of the place for a sociable woman.

18 Oh, Come to the Church

High on the hill, the steeple called,
its bell across the land.
Hearts within disquiet walled,
reached out to meet a hand.

"Oh, I hope Marion will be there!" Carol said, picturing a hoped-for welcome. The ladies and children from the former home had given attention and warmth that added so much to attending church back in Clear Lake; and one little girl was Carol's hope for the same thing here.

As they drove the 'thirty-seven Ford toward the white church high on the hill, with its steeple the highest point in the community, there were mixed feelings among the Watrud family. As they drove up into the church yard, Ida noticed there were cars there but no one going into the church. "We must be late." she spoke, doubtfully. "I thought we had the time right."

Clarence, attempting to raise the family spirits, suggested cheerfully, "Well, we may as well see what we're late for."

So they gathered their jackets and scarves around them and climbed up the front church steps. As Clarence opened the door to let the family in, it was apparent that a different language was being spoken. Ida looked around for some indication of what was going on.

There on the bulletin board inside the entry was the schedule: German Service—9:15, English Service—10:15. Quietly backing out the door, the family agreed to come back in—a little less than—an hour. It was one more experience to chalk up to moving time.

When they pulled into the church driveway less than an hour later, the other arriving cars and the double church door opening as people entered was a much more welcoming sight. On the wall of the entry area was an array of boxes attached to the wall, each with a name. Just learning her alphabet, Carol looked to see if W for Watrud was on any of the boxes.

While her brothers shuffled around and waited to go sit down, Clarence noticed Carol's curiosity and remarked, "We'll probably have one later."

Carol didn't see Marion and her family until after the Watrud family was seated. Then, several pews ahead, Carol spotted Marion's blond pigtails and the straight, neat center part of her hair. Carol's heart filled with an excited hope that they could see each other after the church service. So, lined up in their pew, like six stairs steps, the Watruds attended their first service at Silver Creek Church.

After church, there were a few introductions. Carol was struck by the tall, strong-looking mother of four strapping men, a family of mechanics and truck drivers who lived near the church. Elegant in a rural way, she was both cordial and commanding. Carol soon learned that most of these people were from a common industrious German background and related to each other.

For now, playing with Marion was priority, and much too brief. Marion's round glowing cheeks and merry laugh were a forecast of good times to come, and she and Carol were allowed to play for a few minutes while their parents talked. Then it was time to head for home following promises to see each other soon.

The Dietrichs, Marion's family, lived nearly straight across from the church, and just down the road was the schoolhouse with tantalizing swings and teeter-totters in the yard; but today they drove right by. The Dietrich family with Marion and three little brothers were so cute walking the short distance up their road.

The Watruds passed Eldon's Store, just on the corner where they turned on the hilly road toward the farm. One mile north, then into their muddy driveway, and another mile into the yard. Again. Carol and LeRoy agreed that the view of the deep valley and creek was worth the muddy drive. Carol and LeRoy raced the older brothers up the rickety stairs of the porch to see what was cooking for dinner. Roast or stew in the oven was always so good after being away, and Mama knew how to work with the temperamental oven to be sure it would come out right.

Dad had picked up the Sunday paper at Eldon's Store as a special treat for their first Sunday in the new place.

An even bigger surprise greeted them the following morning. Licky, the gray female cat had gotten into the house and had a litter of kittens in the boys' bed. Mama patiently found a box and old cloths to make a bed for them until they could go to live in the barn. The boys still had to get dressed, eat, help get the cows in their stalls, and walk to school. Thankful that Carol was sleeping late, they all went about their business.

The house had not been put in order totally yet, partly due to lack of places to put things. But the downstairs, one big room with the little adjoining bedroom and pantry, was set up for cooking and eating. The one big room upstairs had been sectioned off for bedrooms by stacking the boxes of belongings and arranging the pieces of furniture in rows, with beds on either side of the lineup.

All quiet in the house. Clarence and Ida, glad the boys had the cows in place for milking, settled down to milk the cows. With three-legged stools and shiny, clean pails, the ringing "squish, squish, sounded through the quiet barn, as milk filled the buckets, and a hungry cat or two waited for the small share that might be poured into their makeshift dish as the milking of a cow was finished and the milk poured into the strainer to fill the cans.

After milking a couple of cows each, Ida jumped up. "I'll go and check on Carol!" Their sleeping daughter suddenly took precedence over the pace of finishing chores.

"Clarence! Clarence! She isn't in her bed. I've looked all over the house, and there's no sign of her." Clarence quickly hung up his stool and pail and hurried to join Ida in searching for Carol.

Wishing they had awakened her, both parents were struck by the thought of the creek at high level from spring thaw and of the little girl's fascination over the beautiful valley. Calling Laddie to go with them, they negotiated the steep hill down toward the creek, calling and peering between brush in hopes of seeing her.

Scouring the whole hillside with no success, Clarence decided he would have to take the car and get neighbors to help with the search. Not having a telephone was a source of chagrin, as they agonized over what to do. Ida would continue to walk the other way from the farm buildings in hopes of spotting their little white nightgown-clad girl.

Ida returned to the house for one more quick look around for the missing child. "Clarence! Clarence!" she shrieked.

A bewildered little girl awoke and burst into tears at the shouting. Ida quickly caught up Carol in her arms, but the child was not yet ready to explain. As Daddy burst into the house, it was apparent that it would take a little time and calming before the truth was known. Carol's little mop of blond ringlets nodded toward Daddy as another torrent of tears erupted. "I wanted to sleep in the bassinet!"

The bassinet, long since outgrown, but kept for any future babies among the relatives, was occupying much-needed space among the boxes of belongings. Carol had spied it under the boxes and crawled in and fell asleep.

Soon, filled with warm food and bundled up in her "chore" clothes, Carol took her place in the barn to watch the completion of the milking. Many a loving and grateful glance was cast her way, and her brothers were greeted with the news of her "rescue" after school. Much diligent overseeing took place as the little four-year-old learned the ropes.

19 Clover Leaf School

Foursquare, red brick, roof sturdy tin,
standing on the hill, dignified.
nearly two acres, two sides fenced in,
with teeters, swings, also a slide.
No outhouses? Amazing that day and age,
ingenuity at work, new that bygone year,
The school founders and builders, so sage,
used sanitary disposal we would cheer.

"You do not have to be able to touch the electric fence to be big enough to go to school!"

Carol's older brothers got a kick out of her eagerness to start school, and they kidded her almost mercilessly. Torn between calling them on their deception and telling Mama, which would displease them so they wouldn't want to play with her, she gritted her teeth and touched the fence. It was a jolt, but gone was the requirement held over her head.

The two years between the move to the farm and the time to be ready for first grade had sped by: three springs of flower picking, summers of berry-picking, and getting to know a few other children who were friends of her brothers paved the way for entering that brick building where eight grades would meet for learning, sharing recess time, and planning holiday programs of drama and music.

Carol's first teacher was Mrs. Plahn, Ida's kind and pleasant friend. Her daughter Marlys was Carol's age, and the disappointment that she attended school in a different district was softened for Carol by the opportunity to play together during infrequent visits.

Carol had had a peek at Clover Leaf School while attending her brothers' school programs, but now it was school for real. In the middle of the big square school yard on the hill stood the solid red brick building with big double doors and a broad staircase inside leading up to a wide hall.

To each side of the staircase was a narrower set of stairs leading down, one to the boys' and one to the girls' indoor toilets. The stairs on the left also led to the furnace room and the main part of the basement.

The big attraction, however, on that first official day at school, was the classroom and Mrs. Plahn, who greeted them with her warm smile. There were rows of desk of various sizes, with seats attached. Those nearest the teacher's solid desk were the smallest and had flip-up seats. "Those must be for first graders," Carol reasoned. Mrs. Plahn kindly took her hand and showed her where she could place her new crayons and tablet in one of the desks—"your special desk"— Mrs. Plahn explained.

Two years went by uneventfully. Two little girls and three little boys passed into grade two, the girls characteristically really "into school" and it subjects, the boys a little less enthusiastic and more full of monkeyshines. The second spring all three boys passed "on condition," with much instruction and direction from Mrs. Plahn, as to how to succeed in grade 3. It was announced, however, that there would be a different teacher the following year.

The next several years Marion and Carol were the only two in their grade, except when an occasional renter would move into the community and enroll children for a year. Days of working and playing marched on; Saturdays were Bible school day. Sleepovers between the two girls were times of giggles and fun; berry picking in the summer tested their determination.

Selling Christmas cards was memorable when both Marion and Carol giggled so hard as they headed back to Dietrich's that they both, after rolling in giggles by the road, had to get dry snow pants, with Marion loaning Carol a pair before she could walk her mile home.

The next summer, although she was still too young to join, Carol was allowed to be an honorary member of the 4-H club, as Clarence volunteered to be leader. That same year, the Watruds began excavation for an addition to the old house, and with Grandpa Watrud and Harold Eldon's help, they were able to close in the basement with a sub-floor for the addition. To Ida's joy, Clarence had piped water from the farm building to the house, with a faucet in the new basement—the closest she had come to enjoying running water!

That summer started out full of farm work and fun 4-H activities; but before long, the Watrud children contracted whooping cough. By the time school started in the fall, all four of them were skin and bones from coughing and gagging for weeks before it cleared up.

With Grandpa's carpentry help, the shell of the addition was erected before snow fell. Anticipation grew strong for the possibility of Mama finally having the house she had hoped for. After all, they had gotten the telephone and electricity over the past four years. Perhaps this would be the year for Mama's newly remodeled house.

Carol loved to be warm, and she often perched on the little wood box behind the cook stove. "I hope you marry a man who can give you a warm house," aunts Edna and Christine remarked more than a few times. Big smiles, she didn't mind the cold when running after her brothers to go sledding.

The years at Clover Leaf were both good and some not so good, but full of memories, unique to the time and place. The building itself was a wonder. The industrious German people had built it solidly and with many distinctive features—one the waste disposal system. A thick concrete-partitioned part of the basement of the building was a fireproof cell where wastes from the toilet accumulated for half the school year, kept odor free by chemicals. The floors of the bathrooms and the columns that held the seats were fireproof steel that could be sealed off with the removal of the seats and steel covers bolted tightly in place. The smoke was directed to the chimney and all the waste was burned during vacation.

Other parts of the basement held the wood room, the play room, a room with a pump, a water jar, and place for lunch preparation, which mainly involved just warming a drink to go with the bucket lunch. A small stairway led up from the play room outside as a fire escape.

The arrangement of this basement led to some fun times and many infractions. One of these latter Carol never forgot. The room behind the furnace room, which was a short corridor to the space under the toilets, was closed off by fireproof doors. It was forbidden and mysterious. During some of the fore-mentioned infractions, this little closed-in area, known as the "skelligan room," became the guard house or prison for the losers in the battle games.

Its purpose was for children to put the unfortunate losers in it. This they did and then ran away. The door from the furnace room led to the stairway that passed the girls' restroom. They would race down the stairway and hall in a kind of mass tag.

On this occasion, the children heard the teacher's footsteps headed their way, and those who could escape unseen, did. One poor little girl, Doreen, was left behind the door, and students who hadn't heard the teacher's approach held the door tightly, ignorant of the fact that Doreen's fingers were crammed between the door and frame. The teacher saw blood on the outside of the door, freed poor Doreen, and called her parents. Doreen's parents didn't answer the telephone, and (hard to fathom) Doreen was sent home, walking the half mile with her injured hand wrapped in a towel.

Swings, teeter totters, games of cops and robbers, and softball were the more acceptable playtime activities at Clover Leaf School. On the swings, called "giant-strides, children would gain momentum as they held hand grips and propelled themselves forward with thrusts of their feet around a steel pole. Always, in every activity, the rule was to stay off the woodpile.

The following summer, the Watrud family again listened for the Kentucky Derby, and Carol ran errands for Daddy as he planted his crop of hybrid seed corn. Teenagers, some nieces and nephews, and some neighbors came to detassel the corn; hay was cut and stored, and the corn crop picked.

20 Life's Difficult Turns

As church bell chime
and prayers ascend,
we cling to time,
Hope is our friend.

Mama, the children were informed, was expecting a baby, probably due in March. She had been sick with asthma and other problems and was to have bed rest. LeRoy and Carol were assigned to keep up the house and dishes. LeRoy, a responsible twelve-year-old, had learned a bit of baking and was able to keep up his part. Carol, with the novelty of having LeRoy to herself, had to be reminded often that this was not all play time. All in all, Mama did get attentive care from the children.

As December rolled around, it seemed the family's close supervision and care were not enough to allow Ida to carry on at home. Regretfully, she told the children she would have to go into the hospital.

During the prayers at the church that Sunday night, Carol remembered other public prayers, prior to the death of a neighbor lady.

Each day, Daddy and Aunts Agnes, Christine, and Edna would convey the news of Mama's condition. One day, Daddy came home and said the little baby had come three and a half months early and had not made it. Carol was sad, but mostly was anxious to have Mama back home.

The next morning, Aunt Agnes came to the house with tears in her eyes. Carol, thinking Aunt Agnes was crying over the loss of the baby, tried to reassure her. "It's all right, I know about the baby."

Gently Aunt Agnes said, "Mama has gone to Heaven."

Ida's older sister Christine, and younger sisters Agnes and Edna, took Carol to the store with them to pick a pretty dress for Mama's funeral. It was only about a week before Christmas, so the store clerk assumed the dress was for the holiday. "Your sister will be pretty in this dress for her party," she cheerfully remarked.

As the family held back tears, Aunt Christine was the first to find her words. "This sister won't be having a party."

All these scenes were etched on Carol's mind, but, still, she was honored to be part of the sad preparation. Three days later, the family stood in a frozen cemetery, in a freezing drizzle, and said goodbye to Mama.

Life would never be the same. Except for a few months from time to time, when a housekeeper was hired temporarily, Carol became the cook and housekeeper for Daddy and three older brothers. She was so young.

21 Skipping and Stumbling

Again, a sad parting,
challenges new,
"ups and downs" roller coaster
comes and leaves view.

What a blessing were all those Hanson relatives, who shared those big, jolly Christmases and were willing to be on hand to help even more than was welcome. Clarence, stinging from the feeling that he had let Ida down by allowing her to endure such a hard life, hesitated to allow her family to step in. There was one exception:

Aunt Agnes offered to keep house temporarily to help the children get back on their feet. A mother figure in the house was wonderful, but Agnes' physical problems of severe rheumatoid arthritis, along with the challenge of trying to keep up with teens, as well as Clarence's conscience (as though he could have prevented Ida's illness) indicated to everyone it was time for that beloved aunt to return home. But the whole family was grateful for the generous lift she provided, and her cheerful expressions and words stayed on their hearts.

In the difficult months and years following Ida's death, Daddy's humor and wittiness, as well as his affection, were a very stabilizing force in Carol's life. He was also at times a stern disciplinarian, especially toward Carol's brothers, which seemed to bring out a "mother hen" attitude in her.

The Watrud relatives, as well, offered cheeriness and welcome visits. Grandpa Watrud was now living near Chetek, Wisconsin, making him available to help with the finishing of the house addition they had started. One aunt's offer to take LeRoy into their home to live with them, was met by a furious reaction by Carol. No one was to take her closest brother! No matter how kind the gesture may be, it is likely to be spurned when close relationships are not taken into consideration.

The tall gambrel-roofed house on the hill began to broaden out as walls and siding topped the beautiful split fieldstone foundation Harold Elden had built. He and his wife (who had played the organ at the funeral and would play at significant events in the future) ran the neighborhood country store. She was a Dietrich by birth, relative to many of the German families in the community.

After the first of the year, the Hanson family had recruited a wonderful nineteen year old married woman, a shirt-tail relative, who was expecting a baby. This was an instant hit with Carol. Her clear expectations of Carol's duties and willingness to help Carol groom herself in a ladylike way were a great addition to the warm-hearted training Carol had received from her mother, Ida.

Betty shared with Carol that she had lost a six-month-old baby on her way home from Europe where her husband Ernie had been stationed in World War II. With this knowledge, Carol loved her fiercely and would have fought a buzz saw to protect her.

Betty's husband came with her as a hired man. Conflict between him and the teen-aged boys soon made the arrangement difficult. While Carol was basking in the delight of helping Betty make hair bows, a vanity skirt, and bedspread from print fabrics, Clarence and Ernie were having their discussion, which finally resulted in an ending of the couple's employment on the Watrud farm.

It all came to a head the night before Carol's eleventh birthday. Carol's brothers had gone sledding two miles away, and Carol was crying that, due to the below zero weather, she hadn't been allowed to go. Within an hour of the brothers' leaving, Carol was throwing up and running a fever.

Carol's sickness didn't prevent the imminent separation. Before the three boys had returned from sledding, Betty and Ernie had packed their belongings and. were gone. Carol's tears, moments before for her missed sledding disappointment changed to sorrowful tears over the loss of a dear friend and mother figure. When her brothers asked her why she cried, she said, "I loved her." The boys didn't understand, and went on their way with simply a shrug.

In the morning, the fever was not gone, and Carol was peppered with stinging, itching spots of chicken pox. Daddy went to town to buy salve to relieve the discomfort and a new record player with long play and record changing capabilities. Within two days, Jimmy also came down with chicken pox, and after a short time of recovery, the two were put in charge of the household chores of cooking and dishwashing. Dane and LeRoy soon came down with the chicken pox as well, and now there were more house helpers than chore helpers for a few weeks.

Carol was finally cleared of quarantine and back in school just two days before she came down with measles. Like the chicken pox, the measles went through all four children. It was later remembered as the winter and spring of rashes.

In the brief periods between rashes and fever, Carol had secretly dug out tiny satin baby shoes that her mother had put away for the baby she was expecting and sent them to Betty for her new baby.

Later in the spring, one of the Watrud aunts spoke to a lady named Mary, thinking she might be willing to keep house for the young family. She did come and worked for four or five weeks; then her son needed her help on the farm. Carol did not really grieve because she had been horrified when Mary had euthanized a nest of baby mice by dropping them in the burning cook stove.

22 Growing Lifescape

Blackberries display shiny fruit,
like gems among the thorns
reminding us that sweet's disguise,
the painless effort scorns.

"They won't break my heart. My children will be nice." Carol was reacting to the kindly words of Grandpa Hanson, Mama's beloved father, who was still cautious in his approach to his talkative little granddaughter, since the death of her mother. Carol was not so little anymore, eleven years old and trying to find her way after the loss of her beloved mother— her friend, guide, cheerleader, and confidante. She and Grandpa both shared this loss, but were expressing it in different ways.

Grandpa was a big quiet, soft-spoken man with a white handlebar mustache and bushy white eyebrows to match. Carol was dramatically proclaiming to him her plans to have six children, and it wasn't so easy for Grandpa to draw her back to reality.

"You know you'll have a husband to do for, and you'll be very busy with all those children."

"I won't have a husband, and the children will be my friends. They will look out for each other like LeRoy and I do."

Grandpa sighed and continued to drop blackberries one by one into the shiny pail. This little chatterbox had been Ida's "Sunshine girl," and she was certainly lovable; but, unlike her mother Ida, who had quietly awaited the outcomes of their activities or plans, Carol's chatterbox plans ran a mile ahead. And, how Carol longed to lean on him and feel his closeness, but she didn't know what to do with the quiet spaces in life. She found herself filling them all in with words. And Grandpa didn't always know what to do with those words.

As Carol and Grandpa left the blackberry patch, smiling together as they held the briars aside for one another, each held dreams of continuing and deepening those moments of closeness somehow.

Reaching the house, with no dear daughter to greet Grandpa and no dear Mama to greet Carol, the two parted company. Carol offered to hold Grandpa's black buggy horse, Babe, as he picked up the lines, preparing to head out on the four mile drive home.

Agnes, his crippled daughter waited for those berries to make jam and can sauce in jars and process them in her deep, blue canner.

Carol skipped into the house there on the hill. Would LeRoy be waiting to help her can her part of the berries? She shook off her unfulfilled longing for the closeness to Grandpa and wandered out on the wooded hill to look for LeRoy.

"It's so beautiful out here, and I can run and jump over little logs like a deer. If it wasn't for Mama being gone, I would want to stay eleven years old forever."

All these mixed feelings were brought together pleasantly by LeRoy's return. Always ready to put an understated lightness on the situation, he suggested it would "be less work if we just ate all the berries." Since that wasn't LeRoy's way, she knew it was jesting. She yelled in silly protest, and LeRoy pleaded in like silliness, "Oh Carol, just string along with me."

"With no rope?" she replied.

"You got me that time." Carol basked in the pleasantness of LeRoy's giving her credit for a bit of wit.

Berry jam made, it was time to get the cows. Another walk in the hills and across the creek with a dear brother—another reason to want to stay eleven—even if that would mean she never could have the six kids.

Blackberry season was at its peak, and that meant it would draw quickly to a close. So, about ten days later, Grandpa pulled into the long driveway in his buggy for the final picking of the season. His horse Babe's lively clip-clop and jingle of her harness heightened Carol's delight in the visit. Then too, this time Grandpa had brought Carol's cousin Bernard, who was about a year and a half younger than Carol with him. Carol, who didn't often get to spend time with cousins, was very excited.

As Grandpa prepared to go out to the berry patch again, he put on an extra belt on which to fasten the handles of the berry pails. Carol, always so excited over her privilege to ride Bud, the big gentle gray horse, offered to let Bernard ride with her and carry the pails. As she mounted and reached down to help Bernard mount, she asked Grandpa if she could carry his pails.

Grandpa waved her on, saying only, "Be off with you, then." In her excitement, it had not occurred to Carol that this arrangement left Grandpa out. There were the two cousins together on the horse, with still-grieving Grandpa walking along behind! The berry picking was fun and profitable, and though Carol and Bernard led Bud home rather than riding him so the berry pails wouldn't spill, Grandpa still walked back to the house in silence.

Carol withered inside, blaming herself that she had lost another chance to get close to Grandpa. "How could I have been so thoughtless?" she lamented, and she mourned inwardly that Bernard would be with Grandpa as he drove Babe to his home, while she would have to stay home.

Strange turns of events increased the distance between Carol and her grandfather and lessened the likelihood of the gap being bridged. A few weeks later, Bernard and his sister Bethynne had a pretend birthday party in the haymow of the barn where their dad Carl kept his milk cows. Not realizing they had not completely extinguished all their merry little candles, the two children went in for supper and then bed.

A few hours later, Carl and his wife Pearl were awakened to the smell of powerful, smarting smoke coming through their window. Rushing into work clothes, they shouted for the younger brother and Grandpa, and they all waged a desperate effort to save the livestock. They saved all but the bull who was enclosed in a very sturdily secured pen far into the blazing area. Grandpa's horse Babe was rescued, but his beautiful vintage buggy was destroyed.

23 Small Town Distance

Fishing, berry picking,
toy construction
Out of our sphere
through many mile's obstruction

Although the Hanson family hurried the progress of building shelter for the cattle and setting up a makeshift farming operation, it appeared that it would be better for Grandpa and Agnes to be in town with Harold, Grandpa's tall, husky third son who was dark and slightly balding.

An inventor ahead of his time, Harold was a blacksmith and a machinist. So, before winter thoroughly set in, Grandpa and Agnes moved in with Harold and his teacher wife Velores, their two little girls, and a baby son.

Grandpa spent much of his time making little wooden bow-guns for grandsons and doll furniture for granddaughters. As Carol noticed this, she cherished all the more the doll cradle he had made for her when she was four. When pictures were passed around now, it always seemed to Carol that Grandpa was with other grandchildren.

There was much change over the course of that winter. The previous winter, Dane had talked his dad into adopting a puppy who was the result of their dear old Laddie's straying to the neighbor's German shepherd, Queen. Though his face was more slender, the puppy had much of Laddie's markings, white with brown sides to his face and a brown spot on his back.

Laddie was slowing down, losing his hearing vision, and it just made sense to have a replacement for him.

A bittersweet feature of the summer was the running water and plumbing progress. Mama had always dreamed of a nice kitchen with plumbing and running water. As the work progressed and became a reality, the family thought of Mama and how much convenience the bathroom would have given her. They comforted themselves with the reminder that she did have the built in cupboards in place with a cornice around the double window that Clarence had designed in a scroll pattern. She had loved that part of the kitchen.

The water had been piped into the house the previous fall via a trench from the well pit to the new basement. Work was underway as soon as the weather warmed up a little, and a pit was dug for the septic tank. The fixtures and cast iron pipe were assembled inside the house, and the soil pipe was trenched out to the septic tank pit.

By the time the pit was finally finished and the septic tank brought to the site night had fallen, and the setting of the tank had to be postponed until daylight. Everyone was exhausted and went to bed, assuming Laddie had stayed in the barn with Prince, the new puppy. The moment the early June sun rose the next morning, Carol and LeRoy raced out to check on Laddie. When they didn't find him in the barn, they looked for him closer to the house.

The search ended at the septic pit; their beloved Laddie had fallen into it and died sometime in the night. Carol and LeRoy sobbed together through the double-edged grief of losing their precious dog on the very spot where Mama's dream was being realized after it was too late for her to enjoy it.

24 High School Days—Finally

While tribulation
patience earns,
in the shorter view,
excitement burns.

Summer passed. Cousins and neighbors had detasseled corn, and the beautiful neighbor teams of horses had been driven in with hay wagons to transport the grain pitched up from shocks in the field to the threshing machine. The dome-shaped pile of shimmering golden straw mounted up as the grain carriers filled bags from the machine's chute and carried them to the grain bins. Neighbor ladies helped Carol cook and serve the dinner to the threshers.

Bessie, an elderly lady bothered by diabetes, had tried her hand at keeping house for the busy family, but it was too much for her health, so school started that fall without household help. The family had pretty much resigned themselves to Carol's cooking, and with Mrs. Friday, a neighbor, to help with laundry, they made do.

After spending his post-elementary school year helping on the farm, Dane was finally able to start high school. He was grateful for the opportunity, and he made an effort to take part in athletics and Ag projects, as well as keeping up with his farm chicken and egg cash projects.

Jimmy was designated to stay home a year as Dane had done following his eighth grade year, following the suit of older cousins.

LeRoy was the more quiet school mate brother and stayed out of trouble, neither instigating nor borrowing it.

When the intermediate grade girls decided to play rodeo, Carol was all in. She had always tried to emulate Caddie Woodlawn of pioneer fiction, and this was a perfect opportunity. The girls harnessed belts around shoulders and waists, playing like they were driving horses to round up the girls who were designated as cattle. Carol got the bright idea of borrowing one of Dad's calf ropes as a lasso to make it more realistic. Everything was lively fun and seemed fine until the teacher, Mr. Heinecke, caught Carol by the arm and pulled her to the side.

Now, this was not the first time Mr. Heinecke had caused Carol humiliation and dismay. The previous year, prior to Carol's mother's death, Carol had requested to use the bathroom during school. Mr. Heinecke didn't allow her to go, until finally Carol wet her pants, and he sent her home. When she returned home, her mother had to bite her lip as she counseled Carol to never allow someone to prevent her from using the bathroom when the need arose. Carol couldn't quite figure out how that would work if the situation came up again at school.

Later, on Carol's first day back at school after her mother's funeral, Mr. Heinecke took Carol aside and admonished her, "Now you need to know there will be no special treatment because your mother died. You will be treated like everyone else." Feeling as though salt was being rubbed into an open wound, the chatty little girl kept her silence and longed for the day to be over.

Another time, this same teacher had grabbed a boy named Donald by the back of the neck, injuring his infected mastoid. Some disrespectful boys referred to his manner of detaining students as the "Heinecke hold." So, when Mr. Heinecke grabbed Carol's arm, fear and anger rose up in her all at once. Without a word, Mr Heinecke snapped her across the back with the rope.

"Now you know how it feels to be hit with a rope like you did," he accused.

Startled by the suggestion that she had been hitting, Carol replied emotionally," I just lassoed. I didn't hit!"

Mr. Heinecke struck her several more times, while the school kids stood transfixed, either afraid to respond or believing that she actually had hit. When Carol started to cry, Mr. Heinecke commanded, "You stop your bawling."

The pain, confusion, and humiliation were almost more than Carol could bear. Forgetting propriety in the extremity of her situation, she retorted, "Shut up!"—words never allowed at home. Mr. Heinecke again grabbed her arm and roughly jerked Carol into the school. Inside the school, he slapped her, commanding, "Say you're sorry."

"I'm not sorry—you're the one who did wrong!" Carol responded in pain and humiliation to this outrage. This was repeated several times: Slap… "Say you're sorry"… "I'm not sorry!"… Slap… "Say you're sorry"… "I'm not sorry!"…, etc. Finally Mr. Heinecke left Carol alone in the building with to "Get over it."

At the end of that long day, Carol and LeRoy jogged home, hoping there was nothing worse to come. Neither Carol nor LeRoy wanted to cause pain to their dad or ignite a scene too fearful to contemplate between Dad and Mr. Heinecke, so they never mentioned the terrible event at home. In later years, as Carol reflected on the bits and pieces she knew of Mr. Heinecke's own broken and somewhat abused life, she remembered anew the truth of the statement, "Hurting people hurt people."

A new teacher entered the picture at Clover Leaf School. Mrs. Steffen was a capable and business-like woman with a growing family of her own. Her motherly instincts flowed over into Carol's life, as Mrs. Steffen attempted to help her with grooming practices. While the Watruds were clean and neat, Carol had her own ideas about style, and the differences between Mrs. Steffen's and Carol's ideas brought Mrs. Steffen a degree of frustration.

Carol treasured the dresses Daddy bought her for each birthday and Christmas, and hand-me-downs from older cousins comprised most of the remainder of her wardrobe. Lovely Aunt Anita, Daddy's youngest brother's wife, would style Carol's hair, cutting it to blend with the natural wave once or twice a year when they could get together.

Several other changes came about that fall. A very large family from Indiana moved into the neighborhood. With decided southern accents, they were charming in their way. Although Nella and Della were twins, they attended different schools, as Nella was already in high school. Their eighth grade brother Ray was dark and handsome and something of a young ladies' man. There was also sixth grader Jimmy, fifth grader Thelma, fourth grader David, second grader Bobby, and first grader Rosalie. This family brought opportunities for new friend making for the Watruds, and the cops and robbers and other games were livelier than ever.

Mrs. Steffen felt the new liveliness as much as anyone.

Another change came about shortly after Christmas. Clarence answered a position-wanted ad in the St. Paul paper for a housekeeper. Maebelle, the woman who posted the ad turned out to be a very nice lady who was an excellent cook and housekeeper. She had a son about two years younger than Carol. Having lost his father recently, good-looking and likable Tom had a good bit in common with Carol, though they didn't often talk about it. Tom enrolled in Clover Leaf School, so, with Jimmy and LeRoy, they had quite an entourage traversing the cross country mile to school.

Tom was well liked in school and soon became part of the activities. They tried their skill at skiing to school, although Carol's skis were prone to soak up wet snow and bog down. It was a laughing matter though, and when they tried switching skis, his slippery model went out from under her.

Tommy and Carol would fill their work and play time with developing little serial stories, each adding his or her imaginative ideas. When there was a writing assignment, Tommy was excited for Carol, believing hers would be very imaginative. It was, so much so that Mrs. Steffen remarked, "It sounds too bookish!"

The happy group would pass the Wheeler Place—the Watrud's second farm so named after its former owners—on the way to school and back home. They would stop and feed cattle and play for a while in the haymow. LeRoy and Jimmy were pretty nice company when the weather was bad and going got rough.

Spring thaw brought a measure of danger as it ran through a little dry run creek under the frozen snow. Once Jimmy went through the frozen snow into the icy, rushing water. With everyone's help, he dragged himself out and hid under the hay in the mow while the other kids brought cry clothes from home, three-quarters of a mile away.

Tom, unlike Carol, had been in several different schools earlier in the year following his father's death, and had trouble catching up to the unfamiliar subjects. To Maebelle's dismay, Mrs. Steffen told her at their Mother's Day party that her son would be held back. Maebelle, along with his many classmates who had seen his hard work and had been lifted by his hopeful expression and attitude, were disappointed and displeased.

The situation lightened when Tommy was taken to pick out a promised horse, a beautiful black Morgan he named Beauty, and both he and Carol were given the privilege to choose a calf for their summer 4-H project. Their summer was full, with the horse and 4-H activities.

Beauty was a very obedient horse, except for one little trick. When passing a driveway, if the rider wasn't on guard, she would feint a turn in, wheel around suddenly, and turn toward home. This was bad if you were bareback, because sudden really meant sudden with Beauty, and you were in danger of being airborne when she swung around.

The alternative was the army saddle that came with her—hard, high in the middle, and with a lengthwise opening, perhaps for ventilation. Long rides for a tenderfoot found places other than the "foot" tender. Needless to say, Tommy and Carol learned to be alert when nearing a driveway.

While Tommy and his mother were away for several weeks in California, Dane and Jimmy rigged Beauty up with driving equipment. During that same time, Carol crashed Tommy's bike on their well-known sliding hill.

Late summer, with the fair and forgiveness from Tommy over the crashed bike, was eventful; and school was about the same. Carol got in hot water concerning the Gibsons, the large family that had moved in the year before. An older brother, home from the army, flattered and flirted with Carol. Knowing it was pure nonsense, but feeling important with all the attention, Carol whispered to classmates that it was the eighth grade brother Ray who had done the flirting.

Foolishly unaware that these girls, who were Ray's friends, would tell him, Carol was shocked to hear he had called her a liar, punctuated with several curse words. Seeing the cursing as much worse than her own untruths, Carol wrote him a note saying that, if he wouldn't take back the insults, she would tell the teacher. Mrs. Steffen took the note from Ray and sentenced Carol to two weeks of every recess, lunch hour, and early arrival confined to her desk.

"Could I not have told him I was sorry?" Carol later wondered. Growing up takes a long, long time.

25 You're Growing Up

Little girls laughing and playing,
under the old apple tree,
wonder, lost closeness dismaying,
"What's become of you and me?"

Following the summer months of excitement over Tommy's return, the Watruds and Tommy joined with neighbor kids—the Dietrichs, the Gibsons, and other families in the school district—in hiking and playing. Poling down the creek in the old flat-bottomed boat that Grandpa had found for the older Watrud boys became a new outlet for Carol, Tommy, Marion's brother Dean, Jack and Joan Friday.

It was school again—both exciting as well as a curtailing of the month of freedom. Interests changed, and Carol wanted to talk about the changes, but ended up just playing and not really sharing from the heart. She feared ridicule, which actually did come, and from the one she thought was her closest friend. She was thankful for girls a grade or two back, and there was still fun to be had, with the ever popular chase games keeping the days lively.

The spring following the one that Mrs. Steffen was held in such ill favor for not promoting Tommy, it was reported that she was leaving the district. Carol, who had smarted a bit under Mrs. Steffen's correction and disfavor, was not sad; but Joan, whose self-image had been bolstered a bit by Mrs. Steffen, was very sorry to hear that she was leaving. Joan asked Carol, who had had a little success with her attempts at writing simple poetry, to help her write a poem for Mrs. Steffen as a farewell gift.

Carol, game for a try at anything that involved creative writing, agreed and listened to what Joan had written.

Joan: I love you my dear teacher. I love you with all my heart....What rhymes with that?

Carol: Part would be good. I never thought the day would come when we would have to part.

(By this time, Carol wasn't so sure she should participate, but she had agreed, so it went on.)

Joan: From the schoolhouse to the hillside, I saw my teacher go....What, now, Carol?

Carol: How about ago?

(Joan continued on with a fill-in from Carol here and there.)

Joan: For she left without a warning, as she did so long ago.

Carol: I'm not sure I can do this.

Joan: "You said."

So they walked the mile and a half, filled with trepidation, saw Mrs. Steffen at the doorway, and began to recite the poem. Feeling very uncomfortable by the time they got the first word out, they began to giggle nervously. Forcing themselves to continue to the end, Joan, with her sincere heart, and Carol, resigned to following through, handed her the paper and ran.

Years later, when Carol was grown and she and Mrs. Steffen ran into each other at the doctor's office, Mrs. Steffen remarked to Carol, "You weren't always so nice, were you?" Dumbfounded, Carol could only wonder, "Which time?"

That same spring Marion allied herself with the girls a grade younger, and together they taunted Carol about her sensitive confidences she had shared. Carol never understood why they did this, but only with some maturity can we see the other person's position, or accept that there are other ways of seeing things.

Confirmation classes at Almena, Wisconsin involved carpooling among parents and some socializing with young people from neighboring towns. It was a meaningful year, and Carol, yearning for a true relationship with God, was confused by the pledge that she would always be loyal to a very restricted part of their denomination. Seeing possibilities in her mother's branch of the church, she felt that her promise was insincere.

It was almost time for Carol's confirmation ceremony, and Daddy bought her a new turquoise print silky dress for the occasion. Maebelle had been on a weekend trip to Minneapolis, and she came back with a coral rose faille dress with a Queen Anne collar for the confirmation as well. Which was Carol to wear?

Daddy and Maebelle had entertained possible plans of marriage, but the controversy around the confirmation dress became part of a conflict that ended those plans. Maebelle found a new position, and she left with Tommy, her living room and dining furniture, the lovely ruffled bedroom linens she had given Carol, and the affectionate relationship that had developed between them.

Carol saw cynicism in her Dad's observation that people provide nice things to make themselves indispensable. Her own observation was of ended friendships and an empty house. The old oak dining table was put back in place, new furniture purchased, and Carol was restored to her capacity as chief cook and bottle washer.

26 Grade Eight, Great?

The old brick schoolhouse still the hub,
blonde-haired eighth grade girls at the fore,
back to the old Clover Leaf 4-H club,
Meadow Lark friends, missed once more.

Grade eight brought minor changes. Carol's Brother LeRoy was now in high school and sharing rides with Dane and Jimmy to Clayton High School six miles away. Carol walked the mile cross country through the fall and winter, walking two and a half miles along the road when spring floods made the crossing impassable. Joan and Jack would sometimes join her at the Wheeler Place, where their paths intersected if the Fridays walked cross-country.

From time to time Dane invited Carol to join him on his weekly paper route, which allowed her to spend some time with friends from the Meadow Brook 4-H, who were on his route. This was special because the Watruds had attended Meadow Lark 4-H at Meadow Brook School for a couple of summers when Clarence found himself too busy to lead at the Clover Leaf 4-H.

It was here that Carol had made friends with May Ann and Allen Libby. Allen had shyly received a Truth or Consequences kiss on the cheek from Carol and honored her with an invitation to sit together at the free movies at Reeve, near the Meadow Brook School,

Eighth grade fall brought another new teacher to Clover Leaf School—for a time. A very nice first year teacher, tall and wholesome, got her start among children who had become very naughty, both in behavior and language.

The older boys used whatever profanity they could get by with and tormented the new teacher when they found out she was dating a local trucker. After a short absence due to severe bronchitis, the teacher did not return to the classroom.

She was replaced by a firm, gracious retired male teacher who stated his expectations clearly. "There will be respect, obeying of the rules, no profanity, and a courteous student body."

A boy, giggling, called out, "Pro-fanny"—once. It was a pretty good year. The new teacher, Mr. Kahl, farmed in his spare time, and his wife, a retired teacher, filled in during his short leaves for farm work. This was a delight to many, as she was a good musician and song leader.

Sanity was established, as the two eighth graders Carol and Marion graduated, less bonded to each other, but ready for high school.

A highlight of that summer was the Barron County Fair, where Carol and LeRoy showed dairy calves. Carol got involved in mischief as some of the kids were washing calves. They started with splashing each other with water on their hands. Soon, they splashed water from small containers. Finally, the fun escalated to full-blown tossing buckets of water. Some of the participants of this "fun" were detained by the police. Carol, by chance, had no bucket in her hand, but Daddy curtailed her freedom of staying at the fair.

The whole summer was full of memories. Riding her beloved paint horse Jeanie, walking the trails along the creek, and climbing a tree from time to time to get a better view allowed for some dreaming.

She laughed as her brothers reported their mishap that took place as they skinny dipped in the creek. They had to cover their lower torsos with mud before they could retrieve their clothes, because the neighbor girl across the creek was watching from behind a rock pile. Having become familiar with riding her horse on the road, Carol would ride the three miles to Gloria's house they sat in the bay window and look at the picturesque little waterfall in the creek.

Never to be forgotten was the evening that Carol and several neighbor girls decided to go swimming by the bridge below the church hill. Changing into their swim suits in the church outhouse, they soon found out that some of the neighbor boys had found out what they were doing and attempted to spy on them. Some girls decided to swim in their clothes.

Singing at the top of her voice as she ran through puddles formed in the grass after a warm summer rain shower, splashing water high, life seemed so good, only missing a dear companion—the one who would someday become first in her heart and life and she in his.

Reflecting on the years she had found comfort and beauty in those beloved hills and woods, Carol thought about the days that eleven-forever seemed good. It was passing, but a long time stretched between that dreamer and the vision of the loving wife and mother of children she would become.

Her future husband would certainly have to appreciate chatty sunshine, if there were to be harmony. Hope ran high in Carol's heart, as there in those Wisconsin hills she dreamed of her tomorrows.

Pick up Carol Morfitt's next in her series;

"Days of Joy, Years of Recovery."

28592527R00074

Made in the USA
Columbia, SC
26 October 2018